M000101283

Organizational Velocity

Organizational Velocity

Turbocharge Your Business to
Stay Ahead of the Curve

Alan Amling, PhD

BUSINESS EXPERT PRESS
Leader in applied, concise business books

Organizational Velocity:
Turbocharge Your Business to Stay Ahead of the Curve

Cover design by 100 Covers

Interior design by Exeter Premedia Services Private Ltd., Chennai, India

First published in 2022 by
Business Expert Press, LLC
222 East 46th Street, New York, NY 10017
www.businessexpertpress.com

ISBN-13: 978-1-63742-242-7 (hardback)
ISBN-13: 978-1-63742-204-5 (paperback)
ISBN-13: 978-1-63742-205-2 (e-book)

Business Expert Press Supply and Operations Management Collection

First edition: 2022

10 9 8 7 6 5 4 3 2 1

For my Mother, Marie-Louise Eveline Amling
She showed me the light so I could share it with others.

Description

If you're not operating with *Organizational Velocity*, you're getting lapped and don't even realize it.

The business environment changes with lightning-fast speed while nimble upstarts cross long-established competitive moats with increasing ease. **The status quo needs to be blown up.**

In *Organizational Velocity*, veteran UPS executive Alan Amling distills five years of research combined with three decades on the front lines of corporate America to reveal a fundamental truth...

Moving at the speed of change is a choice, not a circumstance.

Companies from Amazon to Shaw Industries stay ahead of the curve by operating with Organizational Velocity, a rapid learning paradigm empowering organizations to stay ahead of change.

Amling shows how companies get in their own way and provides pragmatic insights from industrial, digital, and military leaders to **break through the organizational friction and thrive in disruption.**

Organizational Velocity is for current and aspiring executives seeing the disruption at their doorstep but not knowing how to break through the cloud of uncertainty. **So dog-ear the pages and create a company built to stay ahead of the curve.**

Keywords

disruptive innovation; business transformation; senior leadership; competitive advantage; corporate governance; industry 4.0; learning organization; entrepreneurship; culture; organizational bureaucracy; knowledge management; organizational change; data-driven

Contents

Testimonials

"Organizational Velocity *is a sweeping overview of what is needed to fly like a butterfly and sting like a bee in this world of rapid change. Without the wisdom contained in the book, you won't survive."*—**By Richard D'Aveni, The Bakala Professor of Strategy, Tuck School of Business at Dartmouth and author of** *The Pan-Industrial Revolution*

"*Too many organizations fail to survive because their "best practices" were created for a world that no longer exists. Based on his extensive experience managing change at UPS and his research on accelerating adaptation, Alan Amling offers guidance that will help you provoke thought and promote action.*"—**Adam Grant, #1 New York Times bestselling author of** *Think Again* **and host of the TED podcast WorkLife.**

"*Grounded in robust research, brought to life by compelling stories,* Organizational Velocity *is a practical guide to leading through today's uncertain times."*—**Scott D. Anthony, Innosight Senior Partner and author of** *Dual Transformation* **and** *Eat, Sleep, Innovate.*

"*Today's executives know that they should be on the lookout for potential disruptions that could threaten their businesses, but few understand how to spot them or proactively respond.* Organizational Velocity *builds practically and thoughtfully on Clay's frameworks to offer a must-read playbook for leaders who hope to navigate rapidly changing markets and build enduringly successful organizations."*—**Ann Christensen, President at Clayton Christensen Institute for Disruptive Innovation.**

"*In* Organizational Velocity, *Dr. Amling makes a compelling argument for emphasizing technology in the leadership skill profile; a call to action for Boards, CEOs, and all leaders who are building teams and developing talent to lead enterprises in this rapidly evolving digital economy."*—**Jean-Michel Ares, Founder and CEO of Choral Systems, former Chief Technology** and Operations Officer at BMO Financial Group and former CIO at The Coca-Cola Company and GE Power Systems

"The road to success is not for the timid. Every success I've had, from winning the Baja 1000 to making "Act of Valor" to creating next-generation manufac-turing models, has been fraught with uncertainty. In Organizational Veloc-ity, *Alan describes the formula to win when others wilt. Absorb the bumps and bruises that come with rapid learning to break through the gatekeepers and the doubters and achieve your success."*—**Mouse McCoy, CEO Studio MSD, Director, Filmmaker, Former CEO Hackrod and Bandito Brothers**

"Alan Amling's new book is a welcome antidote to the "Maginot Line" defen-sive mentality permeating many modern businesses. His solution, and the only defense that works, is to take the initiative and create opportunities. Busi-nesses that thrive will embody his mantra that "there is no sustainable advan-tage, only persistent advantage, which is cyclical, ongoing, and demands that leaders act amidst uncertainty." Alan's book will show you how to do it."— **By Chet Richards, Author of Certain to Win: The Strategy of John Boyd Applied to Business**

"Technological advances, demanding customers, and disruptive competitors mean that times are anything but business as usual. In Organizational Velocity, *Amling provides a compelling case for how successful organizations are tak-ing advantage of this disruptive era by going on offense, creating velocity to propel their organizations forward. The blueprint provided strongly reso-nates with our experience working with dozens of top companies, and all 21st century leaders would be well advised to use this book as a guide to measure whether their organizations are ready for this new environment."* —**Shay Scott, Executive Director of the Global Supply Chain Insti-tute, Professor of Practice, Benz Supply Chain Leadership Fellow and Ted Stank, Professor, Harry J. & Vivienne R. Bruce Chair of Excel-lence, Co-Faculty Director, Global Supply Chain Institute**

"Organizational Velocity *is a thought-provoking book which should inspire leaders across industries to take action in their organizations. Alan dives deep into how we as leaders can change our way of thinking to make a real and lasting impact on our teams, products, and industries—a must read for those wanting to drive transformation at pace."*—**Gil Perez, Chief Innovation Officer Deutsche Bank**

"Alan Amling brings to life a profound truth for organizations of any size; moving at the speed of change is a choice, not a circumstance. Organizational Velocity *is packed with actionable insights grounded in deep research and personal experience. Consider it your roadmap for navigating the potholes of disruption."*—**Rick Smith, Bestselling author and founder of CNEXT, Fast Radius, World 50, G100 NGL, and Bionic**

"Adapting to perpetual, pervasive, and exponential change is our biggest challenge for the foreseeable future. Alan Amling's Organizational Velocity *will help you and your team move at the speed of the challenge and thrive in disruption."*—**Lieutenant General William "Burke" Garrett III, USA (Ret), Deputy Commander, U.S. European Command, 2014–2016**

"If you have to limit your reading on impending disruption and how to shape your organization to see over the horizon, respond and thrive—then add this book to the short list. It's rare to have an entertaining and educational book and Dr. Amling hits the mark. He's one of the very few that understand the double edged sword of culture and the role of the board in making sure it's positive and not life threatening."—**Joseph H. Astrachan, PhD, Professor Emeritus at Kennesaw State University, Affiliated Professor with the Centre for Family Entrepreneurship, Ownership Affiliated Professor at Jönköping International Business School (Sweden), Family Business Scholar with the Smith Family Business Initiative at Cornell University, and a visiting scholar at Witten/Herdecke University (Germany).**

"More than ever, organizations must move with speed, innovation, flexibility, and adaptability. Organizational Velocity *is a must read for anyone motivated to improve their organization."*—**Lee McCabe, Operating Partner, AEA Investors LP, former Alibaba Group Vice President, North America**

"Real change is not for the faint of heart or the easily deterred. Alan Amling's new book should be required reading for leaders facing the question of how they should steer their companies through today's uncertainty. Organizational Velocity *exposes the land mines and subtle distinctions in the Leader's frame of mind that sink transformation efforts, demonstrates how successful leaders think and act differently, and provides practical insights for navigating today's volatile business environment."*—**Jack Kennedy, CEO/Founder, Platform Science, Inc., Former Executive Vice President: Operations, News Corp.**

"Alan's insights into what it means to have a learning culture is right in line with what we try to do every day at Shaw. Every event is an opportunity to learn and when you have a culture of learning you ensure there is safety in trying new things. From each event, we learn—which makes us better in the future. Organizational Velocity *adeptly illustrates that unsuccessful projects are only failures if you don't learn from them."*—**Kevin O'Meara, Vice President, Integrated Supply Chain at Shaw Industries**

"In the cyber world the term "zero-day" refers to the fact that a computer-software vulnerability exists, either unknown to those who should be interested in its mitigation, or known, and a patch has not been developed. In Organizational Velocity, *Alan enlightens us on the mindsets that drive organizations and the multitude of ways our mindsets hold us back. He forces us to ask ourselves, where are the zero-day type risks in our personal and corporate mindsets?"*—**Charles Adair, Retired Vice Chairman, BMO Capital Markets, Food & Agribusiness Mergers & Acquisitions**

"Few individuals are experienced in all aspects of the broad dimensions of technology, regional and global markets, organizational change, relationship management, market influence, and pacing of new product and service. Dr. Alan Amling has extensive experience in these matters and reflects on the needed cautions and concerns while being bold about embracing the rapid change that is upon us. Dr. Amling's thinking is itself the product of experience in the rapidly changing global market. Each chapter brings interesting and

engaging insight and perspective—from technology to trust. Organizational Velocity *is a guidebook to addressing the challenges of the 21st century."* —**Benn Konsynski, George S Craft Distinguished University Professor, Emory University**

"Organizational Velocity *builds on author Alan Amling's rich experience and in-depth grounded field research to provide clear and practical advice to managers facing change. His book provides less how-to than reflective advice for managers to consider moving forward in relentless change."*—**Anne Smith, King and Judy Rogers Professor in Business and Head of Management Department at the Haslam College of Business, University of Tennessee Knoxville**

"In Organizational Velocity, *Alan has captured the fundamental aspects of change that challenge every organization, particularly great ones. His insight, grasp of history, and knowledge of timeless principles of competition and success (like those of Boyd and Sun Tzu), along with his candid and humble perspective, make* Organizational Velocity *a thoroughly readable guide to navigating the ocean of rapid change and dangerous, shifting currents of supply and demand that emerging technology creates."*—**Col. Howard Marotto, Colonel, Deputy Commander, 4th Marine Logistics Group, USMCR and Business Director, Additive Manufacturing, EWI**

In Gratitude

I've never bought into the "self-made man" concept. We are all products of a genetic lottery and the people that touch our lives. I'm grateful for every person, every experience.

Much of this book was motivated and informed by my 27 years at UPS. Great relationships and talented leaders buoyed the highs and lows of my career. I'm especially indebted to Ross McCullough, who succumbed to my badgering and let me on his team looking at a new concept called e-commerce in the mid-90s, and Dr. Benn Konsynski, an Emory University Professor and advisor to UPS, who helped open my eyes to what's possible.

I am similarly indebted to my professors and colleagues who helped me navigate a PhD program in my 50s. Any PhD student will tell you how vital their dissertation committee members are to their success. Drs. Torsten Pieper and Joseph Astrachan may have bled red ink on my writing, but also showed me the way forward. They led me to the work of Colonel John Boyd, whose insights are woven throughout *Organizational Velocity*. I was also blessed to have Dr. Clayton Christensen on my committee, who was another seminal influence on this book. That he would devote time to a person he had never met but was in a position to help is a testament to his character.

I also owe a debt of thanks to the thousands of people I've worked with in my professional career and my colleagues at the University of Tennessee. Every interaction forges my unique perspectives, and I'm grateful for all of you. This includes the dozens of people I interviewed for my dissertation and this book. I left every interview on Cloud Nine, feeling I had been given gold nuggets with their insights. I've captured some of these insights throughout *Organizational Velocity* in callouts called "Gold Nuggets" or "Truth Bombs." Key influencers include Jean-Michel Ares, Chuck Adair, Ben Baldanza, Dr. Richard D'Aveni, Darin Dredge, Ric Fulop, Gen. Burke Garrett, Jack Kennedy, David Kidder, Mark Kvamme,

Lee McCabe, Mouse McCoy, Kevin O'Meara, Gil Perez, Chuck Ristau, and Patrick Viguerie.

My deepest gratitude is for my wife, Diane, the bedrock of our family who makes everything possible. I am also in constant awe of our children, Alexandra, Jack, and Sydney. There is no greater joy than watching them spread their wings. Oh, the places you'll go.

Organizational Velocity Primer

Organizational Velocity *noun*
Or•ga•ni•za•tion•al Ve•loc•i•ty
Definition of *Organizational Velocity*

1. A rapid learning paradigm of iterative observe-accept-act cycles moving the organization forward.
   //*Organizational Velocity* is the bedrock of companies built to last.
2. The capability to observe and accept (or not) changes in the external environment, so the firm is prepared to act best at the most appropriate time.
   //Today's retail leaders operate with *Organizational Velocity*.

OV *adjective*
O•V
Definition of *OV*

1. To act with Organizational Velocity
   // *OV* leaders need to live on the edge between radical and acceptable.

Critical Components of Organizational Velocity

Observe

- Use technology to cast a wide net of observation.
- Become comfortable being uncomfortable; explore emerging technologies and business models.

Accept

- Use technology to separate the signal from the noise.
- Block the "blockers."

- Hire/promote diversity of thought to reduce blind spots.
- Create boundaries allowing decision making to be pushed to the edge, closest to the customer.
- Use your Board as an asset, not a gatekeeper.

Act

- Foster rapid learning using a small bets strategy and autonomous teams.
- Align hiring, promotion, and compensation to encourage OV actions.
- "Build snowmobiles"; take stock of your existing assets and capabilities to create new value for your customers.
- Create a compelling narrative that unites a distributed workforce around a common mission.
- Eliminate organizational friction—expand information access, raise spending authority, and reduce time-sucking committees and meetings.
- Build your capabilities, creating new options you can leverage in times of threat or opportunity.
- Celebrate OV actions within your company.

Introduction

Coming Soon Near You

Day in and day out, it feels like we're juggling cotton balls in a
blizzard.
—Colonel Dan Elzie, US Marines[1]

That queasy feeling in your gut is not your imagination. The speed and breadth of change today feels like Old Man Time hitting us over the head with his clock. Fueled by the connecting and thinking technologies of the Fourth Industrial Revolution,[2] new companies with new business models have been displacing incumbents at an unprecedented pace. The average age of the top 10 S&P companies dropped from 100 years in 2010 to 30 years in 2019. Why? With all the well-documented lessons from victims of disruption—books and seminars espousing the latest remedies—and consulting firms standing at the ready, corporate failures should be going down, not up. Right?

As an executive at UPS for 27 years, I struggled with disruption. I was all-too-familiar with roadblocks to bold change faced by thousands of leaders in established enterprises around the globe. I read the books, attended the seminars, and worked with the consultants. But I could not crack the code. Instead of wallowing in the status quo, I began pursuing a PhD at the age of 51 to find answers that eluded me in the corporate world. I approached the disruption dilemma from two perspectives.

---

[1] E. Daniel. August 26, 2018. "Colonel, U.S. Marines." Interview by Alan Amling.

[2] Technologies of the Fourth Industrial Revolution include Biotechnology, Robotics, AM, New Materials, Energy Capture, Storage and Transmission, Internet of Things, Artificial Intelligence (AI), Blockchain, New Computational Technologies, and Virtual/Augmented Reality.

I was a leader living the challenges of innovating in a large, established enterprise. I was also an academic viewing these challenges from a third-party perspective. *Organizational Velocity* shares what I have learned so far on the journey.

My guide on this adventure was the Father of Disruptive Innovation, Clayton Christensen. In one of our early conversations, Clay said, "Alan, you need to realize that God didn't create data. It would be of great service if you could teach other executives that the greatest source of their future success is the data that has not been created yet." I was initially taken aback by this challenge. Data that has not been created yet? Clay was always ten (or more) steps ahead of me. I began to think deeply about all of the multi-year plans I had produced over the years, and I realized my folly. As soon as the first initiative in the first year was launched, it would trigger a series of responses from the external environment that I had no control over. At that point, data that had not been created before our action was taken would determine which steps to take next.

Clay's words now seemed obvious. But not to everyone. Would I have received funding approval if I had said to the senior team, "This is our best guess ... we will likely have to change course after the first six months, and I'll come back to you with an updated request"? Not likely. Corporations are set up to plan and act, not sense and respond. While the long-term planning is essential, executives need to realize that "the greatest source of their future success is the data that has not been created yet." This book is a direct response to Clay's challenge.

 Truth Bomb: The greatest source of your future success is the data that has not been created yet.

My research led me to develop a concept called Organizational Velocity (OV), which I define as "the capability to observe and accept (or not) changes in the external environment, so the firm is prepared to act best at the most appropriate time." As shown in Figure I.1, OV is a rapid learning paradigm of iterative observe-accept-act cycles moving the organization forward.

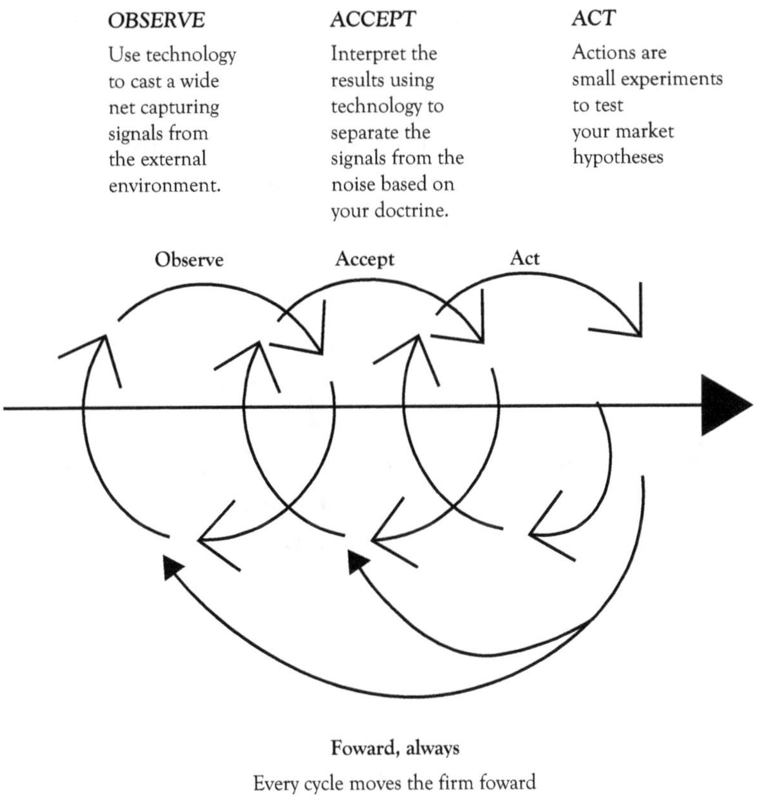

OBSERVE	ACCEPT	ACT
Use technology to cast a wide net capturing signals from the external environment.	Interpret the results using technology to separate the signals from the noise based on your doctrine.	Actions are small experiments to test your market hypotheses

Foward, always
Every cycle moves the firm foward

Figure I.1 Organizational velocity explained

Of the dozens of companies interviewed for this book, the only company excelling in all three areas—Observe, Accept, and Act—was Amazon. Other high-performing companies appear to be on the path to OV and have embraced a learning culture. The firms struggling to find their footing on the shifting sands of the digital economy are typically stuck in legacy mindsets. They may try new things, but their actions are often fleeting.

> Gold Nugget: Organizational Velocity is the capability to observe and accept (or not) changes in the external environment, so the firm is prepared to act best at the most appropriate time.

Financial markets love stability and, consequently, public companies do too. OV ascribes to a worldview that the future is not in our control, but the ability to prepare for it is. This small change of thinking and acting requires a significant transformation most enterprise companies struggle to make. It's one reason that despite the abundant research and practical examples of disruption over the last 20 years, the S&P 500 continues to freefall.

And it boils down to this. The speed at which the change is happening and the fact that the technology that has been created in the last five years allows you to reinvent the business model and create a better solution for the consumer, and the fact that consumers now are not as loyal. You combine those three things; it's happening, very, very fast. You can fundamentally transform the value proposition and the economics of delivery with technology, and consumers will go to the best answer. You can lose your business very fast.

—Jean-Michel Ares—Founder, Choral Systems, Former CIO at BMO Financial Group, Coca-Cola, and GE[3]

The Balance of Power Has Shifted Forever

On January 01, 1983, a new communications protocol was launched that allowed different computer networks to communicate with each other. The Internet was born, but it wasn't until many years later that its full power was used to drive human behavior on a mass scale. Fast forward to 2021. The infamous GameStop short squeeze fascinated investors around the world. How could a band of independent investors coordinate a takedown of several all-powerful hedge funds who were shorting the stock? Eddie Murphy and Dan Aykroyd did it the same way when they brought down the evil Dukes in the movie "Trading Places," which came out the year the Internet was born. The technique is not new. What is new is the

---

[3] A. Jean-Michel. September 02, 2018. "Founder and CEO, Choral Systems, Former CIO BMO Financial Group, Coca-Cola, and GE Power Systems." Interview by Alan Amling.

virtual consolidation of power. Individual investors did not have inside information on a crop report. Still, they consolidated their power to send GameStop shares skyrocketing from $20 per share to over $400 per share while the Hedge Funds clutched their short contracts. Individuals can now do what only the big players could do—put their thumb on the scales of the market.

In the 90s, the Internet gave consumers access to the greatest source of power since the dawn of time, information. The power differential changed. The consumer now dictates the terms. Take buying a car, for example. If the salesperson can't meet my price target, I can say, "I'm walking. I know exactly what they paid for that car and the current incentives available." The Internet allowed us to peer into the black box, which has been shattered into 280 character tweets and Reddit posts. Anybody can know almost anything.

 Truth Bomb: The Internet unleashed the greatest source of power since the dawn of time, information.

The Internet has become an organizing tool. Like any tool, it can be used for good or evil. We cheered the small investors having their day with the GameStop squeeze in 2021 but quailed at the sight of the U.S. Capitol being attacked. The risk landscape has changed. Your company, your industry, is no longer controlled by the largest players but the smallest. Your ability to sense and respond to changes as they occur has never been more important. Your survival depends on it. OV provides a framework for the constant, iterative adaptation required to survive and thrive in the shifting sands of the digital world.

OV is not a business model, technology, or get-rich-quick scheme. It's a way of life. It's a shark moving through the water, continually adapting to its environment. When you stop adapting (known as the status quo in the corporate world), you will die. This has always been true, but recent events have ramped up the urgency for every business.

 Gold Nugget: An OV company is a shark moving through the water, continually adapting to its environment.

As global warming intensifies, flash floods and fires are on the rise; COVID-19 has shown how quickly a virus can bring the global economy to its knees; technology bridges are easily spanning competitive moats; and cyber-hackers are disrupting critical distribution systems. We can mitigate a risk, but we can't plan for all the uncertainty or control the field of play. Access to technology and equipment is no longer a differentiator. Incumbent organizations can no longer persist with a sustainable competitive advantage. Connecting and thinking technologies offered on a pay-by-the-drink basis changed the paradigm of competition. Playing defense is not the answer. There's simply too much coming at you. External disruption, omnipresent in an industry, is nearly impossible to plan for and predict. Technology is part of the solution, but it isn't *the* solution. Leaders must first embrace a different way of thinking. *Organizational Velocity* is about getting to the core of change by challenging our entrenched paradigms and opening the organization to discovery and long-term growth.

The Origins of Organizational Velocity

I sat in my office with my head in my hands after one of the many surreal experiences every corporate manager goes through from time to time. Earlier that day, I reviewed an innovative proposal with my manager to ensure his support one last time before presenting the idea to his C-level manager. That afternoon, the C-level executive did what great executives do, asked great questions. I got to that fateful point when the answer is, "I don't know. We need to learn that and adjust as necessary." It was the response I hoped would open the door to the unknown, to discovery. That is the nature of disruptive innovation. Its outcome is less certain than a sustaining innovation, which is essentially doing what you are already doing but better, quicker, and cheaper.

At that point, it's not about the facts, but it's about conviction. It's about the willingness to sail into new waters, learn, and then pivot. Unfortunately, at the first signs of pushback, my manager seemed to forget we had a meeting that morning. The status quo won again. I have heard similar stories in my interviews with business leaders and discussions with colleagues across the industry spectrum. Unfortunately, we can too often identify the innovators by the arrows in their backs.

This book draws on my exhilarating and frustrating attempts to push forward innovation as a leader at UPS and shares what I have learned from my work in cracking the code of companies built for the long run. I describe them as perpetually self-renewing, Forever Companies. There are no formulas, no "8 Steps to Success" to get there. What worked for one business at one point in time will likely not work for another. And it will never happen without a leader who can envision what their company can become even when the path to get there is not clear. What allows leaders to pivot when other firms, often with more resources, experience, and market clout can't? Is it all about a brilliant strategy? To answer that question, I explored hundreds of academic research articles, conducted dozens of formal interviews, and held countless informal discussions with colleagues around the world. What I found out surprised me. Rather than leading to success, a brilliant strategy often turns out to be the narrative used in hindsight to explain it. Success was a process, not a destination.

 Truth Bomb: Success is a process, not a destination.

Cognitive Barriers, Corporate Control Valves, Accelerators, and John Boyd

I distilled everything I had learned from my research into three categories: cognitive barriers, corporate control valves, and accelerators. Cognitive barriers are the roadblocks we create that slow or stop effective decision making. These barriers take the form of cognitive bias, loss aversion, path dependency, and a myriad of other impulses that keep us acting in character. Corporate control valves are used to regulate the firm. Examples include compensation plans, performance metrics, resource allocation procedures, corporate culture, and organizational learning.

These valves reflect the firm's balance of trust and control (more on that in chapter 5). Accelerators are all the actions taken to become synchronous with the world outside the firm's four walls. These include

Corporate Control Valves
culture, metrics, and rewards,
moderate the amount of
control vs. autonomy in the
firm.

Cognitive barriers
Arise from outdated
mindsets, creating
friction and slowing
down ov.

Accelerators align
external realities to
internal truths,
reducing friction.

Figure I.2 Controlling the corporate growth engine

building new dynamic capabilities, flexible and adaptive systems, and ambidextrous leaders exploring new opportunities while exploiting existing ones (Figure I.2).

All of this was insightful but not pragmatic. What I had learned helped me understand the "what" and "so what" of success in the digital economy, but not the "now what." The "what" came together when I was steered to the works of Air Force Colonel turned management philosopher John Boyd. Colonel Boyd spent the greater part of his life addressing a challenge in the Air Force that many organizations are now facing: survival in a many-sided, uncertain, and ever-changing world. Boyd dug deep into the 2,500-year history of war, beginning with Sun Tzu. After two decades of academic study and military work in the field and at the Pentagon, he synthesized what he learned into a briefing, *A Discourse on Winning and Losing*.[4] The goal, Boyd said, was to improve one's capacity for independent action.[5] To do this, organizations need to "be swift and agile, able to understand the environment quickly, spot opportunities and emergent threats immediately, make decisions rapidly, recognize when change is appropriate, and enact such changes

---

[4] J. Boyd. 2018. *A Discourse on Winning and Losing*, 13. Air University Press, Curtis E. LeMay Center for Doctrine Development and Education.
[5] J. Boyd. 1987. *Destruction and Creation*. US Army Command and General Staff College.

without delay."[6] To accomplish this, Boyd suggested an organic design for command and control with implicit understandings between leaders and troops that allow for cooperation and quick decision making in fast-moving environments.

Boyd's most noted accomplishment is a four-stage cycle of organizational adaptation in an ever-changing, non-linear environment. This cycle is commonly known as the OODA Loop, representing a continuous and non-linear process of *Observation, Orientation, Deciding, and Acting.*

Boyd's insight helped me put all the pieces together: Dr. Christensen's challenge, the academic research, the interviews, and my own lived experience. Rapid change must be met with rapid reinvention. That can only be done through iterative learning cycles driven by direct engagement with the external environment; your customers, competitors, investors, and community stakeholders.

 Gold Nugget: Rapid change must be met with a rapid reinvention.

Companies need to lean in on accelerators, challenge their cognitive barriers, and turn their corporate control valves toward reinvention. To operate with OV, companies must first create a near friction-free environment that allows for accelerated learning and action. Getting there is anything but easy. *Organizational Velocity* will be your guide.

The Tightest Ship in the Shipping Business

Throughout this book, I draw from my time at UPS to highlight the real challenges of transformation faced by many incumbent organizations, both public and private. I highlight the failures more than the many successes because that's where the learning takes place. I'm incredibly grateful for my time at UPS. The company Jim Casey built is still a great

---

[6] J.H. Astrachan, C.W. Richards, G.A. Marchisio, G.E. Manners, P. Mazzola, and F.W. Kellermanns. 2010. "The OODA Loop: A New Strategic Management Approach for Family Business," In *Handbook of Strategy Process Research.* Edward Elgar Publishing.

organization that makes lives better for millions of people worldwide. The issues brought to life in this book are not unique to UPS. I have seen them in companies I worked with over my 31 years in Corporate America and in the hundreds I've researched and interviewed for this book. I use examples from UPS because it's my lived experience.

I worked at UPS during a unique time in its history. I started with UPS in 1994, five years before it went public, and still a founder-influenced company. Managers referred to each other as partners. We started meetings reading from the UPS policy book. After a manager introduced a policy regarding the organization, our people, service, character, reputation, or economic stability, we discussed how the policy applied to today's environment. I was always amazed how a policy written in 1929 was still relevant in 1999. Fundamental truths are timeless. After UPS went public, our focus slowly and steadily shifted to quarterly earnings, typical of a Fortune 500 company. Public market pressures clouded the vision that guided UPS since 1907.

I write this book with the sincere hope UPS will heed its lessons so it can enrich lives globally for another 114 years.

Since you will read some unflattering truths of this experience, let me take this time to share some of the many things that make UPS a truly great global corporation.

It all starts with its humble founder, Jim Casey, an unsung corporate giant who turned a small messenger company in Seattle into a global powerhouse, generating $85B in annual revenue and delivering 25 million packages and documents every day. Three characteristics defined UPS: integrity, community service, and efficiency.

Integrity contributed to employee morale at all levels. Over my career, I rarely saw someone get fired for performance issues. A breach of integrity, on the other hand, was dealt with quickly and severely.

Community service has always been a hallmark of UPS. It's one reason UPS is admired worldwide and why I hope it keeps its standing in the world economy. UPS has selflessly served communities around the world. My favorite example is the Community Internship program, designed to sensitize rising UPS managers to social needs that may go unnoticed. When I attended, we were based at Henry Street Settlement, a community center in the Lower East Side of New York City that UPS has supported since the 1960s. I served in soup kitchens, helped ex-convicts develop resumes, and assisted social servants battling AIDS, poverty, and drug addiction. It forever changed my perspective. UPS doesn't advertise this program or derive any financial benefit. They do it because it's the right thing to do.

Efficiency is another core value of UPS. On my first day, after pointing out my sport coat did not qualify as a suit, my manager explained the spartan offices at UPS. "We don't have wood paneling in our offices so that we can have wood paneling in our homes." "I don't want wood paneling anywhere," I thought, but I understood his point. Sweat the pennies at work so you can have the pennies at home. I was hired into marketing, but I started in industrial engineering, a department driven by efficiency. I conducted time studies to understand the exponential improvements in profit from incremental improvements in driver efficiency and packages delivered per stop.

Over the decades, UPS has demonstrated an ability to transform itself. The original company, American Messenger Service, had to transform when a new technology, the telephone, nearly put it out of business. Since then, the company has transformed several times, and as of Summer 2021, the company is undergoing yet another successful transformation, if its surging stock price is any indication. Is UPS a Forever Company? We'll debate that in the coming chapters.

And You Thought Sunday Was for Sports

I hope OV becomes a tool to help you challenge conventional thinking and encourage your firm to adapt more quickly and effectively to change. I envision you reading this book on a Sunday afternoon as you take time to think about the future of your business. Or, you are reading it with your team around the conference table and discussing one of the friction points slowing down your growth. I've done precisely that with books such as Adam Bryant's *The Corner Office* and Patrick Lencioni's *The Five Dysfunctions of a Team*. They can be transformational as you read them carefully and allow them to change your thinking.

Use this book as a reference. You can read it cover-to-cover or focus your reading on one area that's challenging you. Each chapter ends with a concise summary of the chapter topic (WHAT), its importance (SO WHAT), and recommended actions (NOW WHAT). Use these summaries to create your Sunday thought starters and team meeting talking points.

Here's where we're going: The first two chapters establish the foundational mindset needed for OV to flourish. Chapters 3 to 8 focus on smashing the roadblocks to OV throughout the organization. Chapter 9 revisits the seminal question, "Do you want to live?" and asks, "How then shall you live?" Let's get started.

What?

The balance of power is moving from the few to the many and giving rise to new technology-enabled business models challenging the status quo of established companies.

So What?

Companies are losing their market position at an unprecedented pace. Thriving in disruption requires firms to sense and respond to changes in their external environment with speed and agility. To do this, the corporate control valves need to be tuned to rapid learning and execution.

Now What?

OV was written to help you navigate this journey to becoming a Forever Company. Use the stories and lessons in this book to inform the hard work of real change and create a (near) friction-free organization that thrives in disruption instead of becoming a victim of it.

CHAPTER 1

Do You Want to Live?

The relevant question is not simply what shall we do tomorrow, but rather what shall we do today in order to get ready for tomorrow.
—Peter Drucker

Royal Joh. Enschede was founded in 1703 in the Netherlands as a printer of books and manuscripts. A century later, they were the exclusive printer of Dutch Central Banknotes. Eventually, they became a security printer of notes and stamps for several countries around the world, just as early signs of disruption were peering over the horizon. The Euro was introduced in 1999, and e-mail was slowly reducing the need for stamps. Royal Joh. Enschede knew they needed to change, but pride and pedigree had made them complacent. They stuck their head in the sand and suffered a steep and predictable decline in business. To save itself from bankruptcy, the company was sold to an investment firm in 2014. In 2016, they stopped printing banknotes and were forced to lay off a "significant" number of employees.[1]

This result was predictable; yet, it caught them by surprise. Their past success had blinded management to the requirements for future success. Current examples, such as Blockbuster, Kodak, and Blackberry, point to the same underlying reason. All these companies were disrupted because they were smart and knew their business, not because they weren't.[2] It's

---

[1] 2016. "Printing House Joh. Enschede Stops Printing Banknotes," *Nederlandse Omroep Stichting*, no. 15, p. 10. https://nos.nl/l/2145965 (accessed January 12, 2016).

[2] C.M. Christensen, M. Raynor, and R. Mcdonald. 2015. "The Big Idea: What is Disruptive Innovation," *Harvard Business Review* 93, no. 12; H.C. Lucas, Jr and J.M. Goh. 2009. "Disruptive Technology: How Kodak Missed the Digital Photography Revolution," *The Journal of Strategic Information Systems* 18, no. 1.

an ironic flaw reinforced by childhood experience: if a particular action is rewarded, we should do it again and again. That works as long as nothing in your external environment changes. The rinse and repeat strategy only changes if you discover a better way to earn the same reward or if the person judging your action changes.

 Truth Bomb: Companies get disrupted because their management is smart, not because they aren't.

Consider the classic case of disruption put forth by Clayton Christensen in 1997. He described a process whereby a simpler, more affordable product or service takes root at the bottom of a market. While the incumbent focuses on higher margins at the top end of the market, the upstart hones their offering, eventually saturating the low end of the market and moving upstream to displace established competitors. This has become a well-established pattern that intelligent managers at great companies still ignore.

The Case of Big Brown

As a long-time UPS shareholder, I benefit from the company's success. When UPS announced a new CEO on March 12, 2020, as the COVID-19 pandemic spread across the United States, I was expectantly optimistic. Carol Tomé seemed like a brilliant choice. She was the first CEO in UPS history who did not grow up in the famously promote-from-within company, although she had been a board member for many years while a CFO at Home Depot. Her first earnings call was a breath of fresh air. She talked about her vision, the need for more diversity, and revamping the archaic decision-making processes that had slowed down the company for years. I began to question whether I had retired from UPS too early!

"UPS will be better, not bigger," she said.

The slogan seemed strategic: UPS would "sweat the assets" and focus on the higher-margin verticals, such as health care and small- to mid-sized businesses. She almost immediately raised rates as capacity tightened with the pandemic-driven increase in demand for e-commerce deliveries.

She slashed capital expenditures and sold off a low-margin trucking business. Wall Street cheered, and UPS stock soared to an all-time high. I joined in the celebration.

But, I also cringed. Beneath the surface of her words lay the seeds of disruption: "Better, not bigger" and "sweat the assets" translate, roughly, to reduced investment and a focus on the highest return areas. On the surface, her language makes sense, but it's not the path of a Forever Company, which makes decisions beyond its quarterly earnings and the tenure of its current leadership.

The risk of a "better, not bigger" strategy was familiar. This was the classic "Innovator's Dilemma" outlined by Christensen in 1997. The "dilemma" is whether incumbents focus on existing high-margin segments that are a good match with current capabilities or invest in new capabilities required to capture an emerging, lower-margin part of the market. Christensen's book features the infamous case study of mini-mills disrupting U.S. Steel in the 1970s. Fifty years later, a similar scenario is playing out in the package delivery business. Table 1.1 shows a side-by-side comparison of strategic moves by U.S. Steel in the 1970s and UPS in 2020 and early 2021.

The convergence of broadband, GPS, ubiquitous smartphones, and artificial intelligence allowed Uber to launch an online ride-hailing service in 2009. Online food delivery companies like UberEATS and DoorDash soon followed. While pizza delivery had been in place for years, this new technology-enabled model allowed businesses to tap into a ready supply of delivery vehicles and drivers on an ad hoc basis. It was revolutionary. Deliveries were made within an hour, but they were also haphazard and low margin. Profitability was an aspiration.

Same-day delivery of fast food was a business that UPS and other incumbents had no interest in. It didn't fit UPS's efficient route-based network, and paying gig-workers for delivery would be an uphill battle with the Teamsters Union representing UPS drivers. UPS made the logical choice. They focused on current customers who placed a high value on an efficient global network and were willing to pay more for it.

Fast forward to 2020. E-commerce spikes, outstripping UPS delivery capacity. Retailers increasingly use their stores to fulfill online orders with deliveries that don't need the celebrated national networks of UPS,

Table 1.1 U.S. Steel and UPS: Similar paths?

Characteristic	U.S. Steel circa 1980's	UPS Circa 2020/2021
Incumbents move up-market, abandoning the low-end of the market	Focused on higher margin flat rolled steel and ceded the low margin rebar business to the upstart mini-mills led by nucor	Focused on higher margin healthcare, international, and small/mid-size (e.g. SMB) segments, limited low-margin ecommerce shipments, and ignored emergence of low-margin same-day delivery market
Smaller companies with fewer resources and lower quality product enter market at low end	Nucor, chaparral, florida steel corporation, georgetown steel, connors steel, north start steel–rebar was the entry point	Doordash, postmates (bought by uber), instacart, grubhub, point pickup, gopuff–fast food/Grocery was the entry point
Incumbent invests in upgrading current processes to improve efficiency, cuts workforce	Reduced labor hour per ton of steel from 9 hours in 1980 to 3 hours in 1991 and reduced their workforce about 75% during the same period	Invested over $15 billion in their smat logistics network, executed "fastest ground ever" initiative, offered voluntary buyout packages to thousands of non-operating managers.
Sell or close lower margin business units	Closed part or all of 20 obsolete factories in 1983.	Ups sold low margin ups freight division to tforce freight in 2021.
Competitor moves upmarket	Mini-mill nucor begins producing high margin flat rolled steel in 1989.	Doordash began delivering ecommerce purchases For walmart, macy's, petsmart, CVS and wal-Greens in 2020.
Mainstream customers start adoping the entrants' offerings in volume	By 1980 nucor owned 90% of the rebar market and about 30% of the market for rods, bars, and angle irons. Nucor overtook U.S. Steel in total steel production in 2014 and never looked back.	?

FedEx, or the U.S. Post Office. Options proliferate in every locality, from contractors to gig workers, for local pickup with local delivery. Upstarts like Postmates and DoorDash, which already had a solution for local delivery, rushed in to fill the void and expand their market. Subsequently, Uber purchased Postmates for $2.7 billion in July 2020. A few months later, DoorDash went public, valuing the company at $72 billion.

Meanwhile, as part of its "better, not bigger" strategy, UPS reduced capital expenditures and focused on improving service for high margin albeit slower-growing segments like international and health care while actively shunning some faster-growing but lower-margin e-commerce segments. Delivery capacity was constrained, shipping rates increased, and the rapidly growing same-day local delivery market was ignored.

The disruption was on.

The ostensibly strategic decision to leave the lower-margin business to the startups and the also-rans seemed to be logical, even brilliant. The market value of UPS nearly doubled in the new CEO's first year. But in this case, the logical thing to do may turn out to be the wrong thing. Recent history is replete with stories of companies abandoning lower-margin products and businesses and aggressive startups happily filling the void. The new entrants continually innovate their business models and processes to stay profitable in a low-margin market. Eventually, these upstarts saturate the low end of the market and move upmarket to displace the incumbents with a better value proposition. The pattern of disruptive innovation popularized by Christensen over 20 years ago has played out in dozens of industries, from entertainment and photography to print media and manufacturing. It is now prevalent in health care, education, financial services, and yes … package delivery. If the pattern is so well known, why does it continue? The answer lies in the motivations and mindsets of the leaders who wrestle with the innovator's dilemma.

The question "Do you want to live?" is not merely rhetorical. It's existential: "Am I, as a leader, willing to sacrifice the profitability of the company I lead today to increase its chances for survival in the future?"

If leaders don't open themselves to the possibility of failure, they have to question their genuine commitment to live. If they are not willing to fight and lose some battles, they are not pressing hard enough. Successful organizations lose to win. In the losing comes the learning that moves the company one lesson closer to victory. Any leader ensconced in a relatively stable industry and who focuses on maximizing profit today at the expense of corporate longevity does not really aspire to live.

 Truth Bomb: Successful organizations lose to win.

This book will make sense only if you want to lead your company to thrive beyond your tenure. Beyond next quarter. Beyond your next bonus. The Fourth Industrial Revolution technologies, such as artificial intelligence, the Internet of Things, and Additive Manufacturing, are all accelerators. As they quicken creative destruction, they also create momentum with new opportunities. It's controlled chaos. To live is to focus on what can be, not what was. And not succumb to the seductive strategies that maximize today at the expense of tomorrow.

Creating Opportunities to Live and Prosper

Life presents opportunities that enable us to create more options for ourselves. The decision to go to college does not guarantee success, but it provides more opportunities to be successful. You may never have to use the karate skills you honed over six years of lessons, but you've created the opportunity to do so should the situation arise. An entrepreneur's job is to create options. That takes guts, grit, and support. Entrepreneurs typically have a strong support system of friends and family that enable them to take high risks to bring their idea to life.[3] *The Black Swan* author Nassim Taleb says, "an option is what makes you *antifragile* and allows you to benefit from the positive side of uncertainty, without a corresponding serious harm from the negative side."[4]

Companies are no different. The OV process creates options by helping leaders observe, accept, and act on changes in the environment. Incumbents with existing businesses can nurture the building of new capabilities. Some of these capabilities may create critical advantages that enable future growth. This was the case for Netflix, which began to produce original content as its leadership saw the competitive landscape for streaming become increasingly cluttered. Netflix had already evolved its business model from DVD mail delivery to film streaming. Original content was simply the next phase. As Disney, ViacomCBS, Amazon, and

---

[3] D.G. Blanchflower and A.J Oswald. 1998. "What Makes an Entrepreneur?" *Journal of labor Economics* 16, no. 1.
[4] N.N. Taleb. 2012. *Antifragile: Things that Gain from Disorder*, Vol. 3. Random House Incorporated.

others entered the market, the competition for content has increased expo-nentially. Netflix's investment in production has created the option to live.

Fifty-nine-year-old Walmart behaved like a startup during the pan-demic. Its leadership understood that last-mile delivery is an extension of their "everyday low prices" value proposition. Walmart went on the offensive. Consider all the simultaneous pilot projects and partnerships that Walmart initiated just in the area of logistics in 2020:

- Autonomous delivery with Cruise, Nuro, Udelv;
- Middle mile autonomous delivery with Gatik;
- Last-mile delivery with Instacart, Point Pickup, DoorDash, and others; and
- Experimenting with Dark Stores (i.e., highly automated ful-fillment locations that could theoretically operate in the dark) while increasing same-day Ship-From-Store to over 3,000 locations.

Walmart, of course, has no crystal ball. It's no different from any other incumbent (ergo, successful) company, except in one significant way. Walmart is creating options that allow for quick pivots based on changes in the external environment. Creating optionality is a crucial capability for companies to thrive in a disruptive world.

 Gold Nugget: Creating optionality is crucial for companies to thrive in a disruptive world.

Deadly Efficient

If you say "Yes" to the question "Do you want to live?" then you must also *do* yes. Release your team to create rapid learning opportunities rather than expecting every project to succeed right out of the gate. Encour-age a mindset that incorporates a fail-to-succeed philosophy. At most established companies, an expectation of failing was heresy. UPS was no different; it was "the tightest ship in the shipping business," and lead-ers regularly delivered successful project outcomes. However, while the no-failure bar makes sense for sustaining innovations—adding a new piece of technology to improve a process by 20 percent—it can be devastating for innovations that touch human behavior. Humans are not as predictable as machines, and outcomes are uncertain. Leaders who asked for funding for an uncertain outcome would be branded as having poor judgment: "Why would I give you money and resources if you don't feel confident about your pilot?" No executive would dare propose the company spend money on three similar pilots with the same objective, something Walmart and Amazon do brilliantly.

Too often, the efficiency mantra plays like a symphony in the boardroom.

Every company has a finite set of assets. Every leadership team goes through an exercise quarterly or yearly to allocate those scarce assets to meet their strategic and financial objectives. The executives marshal the financial calculations, which they all learned in business school to help them make a decision: net present value, breakeven analysis, and return on assets/invested capital/equity; the list goes on. Macho talk of "failing fast" and the boondoggles to "blue ocean strategy weekends" belies their true intent to focus those limited assets in areas that will create the greatest return for the company. It's a one-dimensional, simplistic approach to business.

Efficiency works as long as the external environment doesn't change. You can sharpen the knife, and your cuts will go deeper every day. But it's meaningless if you are cutting in the wrong place. An obsession with efficiency will hurt the firm if it continues to be efficient at processes that are no longer relevant. No matter how easy Blockbuster made it for customers to locate a video in their stores, it wouldn't have saved the business.

Some companies, however, decided to live. They made watershed decisions at critical moments that put their collective ass on the line. When Netflix switched from DVD rentals to streaming, customers protested, and its stock plummeted. Instead of retreating, Netflix innovated again and developed original programming. What seems evident in hindsight would never have happened if a leader had not dared to risk the present for the promise of a better future.

When Adobe transitioned its buy-the-software business model to rent-the-software, it upset many investors and left profit on the table. Adobe stuck to its decision, pivoted to the future, and then soared. When Verizon was still just a landline telephone service provider, its executives made bold decisions to move into digital. Instead of following the typical "picking a winner" process and going with it, they let several mutually exclusive networking technologies play it out until it became clear which one was dominant. Verizon's leaders were humble, willing to live in a cloud of unknowing until they did know. When Shaw Industries (a subsidiary of Berkshire Hathaway) diversified from its core carpet business into all types of flooring, i.e., from hardwood to turf for sporting facilities, it risked what it knew to create an entirely different future. PayPal started as a cryptography company; only after an iterative process of trial and error (what can only be described as Organizational Velocity), PayPal found its calling as the default online payment system of millions.

The oft-told story of Apple is worth another mention: in 1997, on the verge of failure, Apple brought back its ousted founder, Steve Jobs, to change direction. Instead of following marginal product ideas down the rabbit hole, Apple began focusing on beautifully designed electronics. This led to the iMac, the iPod, and the iPhone, which create a consumer frenzy every time a new model is released. In 20 years, Apple went from the gates of disruption to being indelibly integrated into the fabric of everyday lives worldwide.

A less-known example is Wolters Kluwer, a Dutch multinational that began as a publishing house in the 1830s. Publishers have been perennial victims of digital disruption, and in 2003 when Nancy McKinstry became the new Chair and CEO, the company still generated over two-thirds of its revenue from print products. Today, digital products make up over 90 percent of revenue, and the stock has soared. According to McKinstry, "It's not moving our results in the current year ... you have to be able to have patience around investing over the long term. Our best-selling products started being built 12 years ago."[5]

---

[5] HBR IdeaCast. 2019. "How One CEO Successfully Led a Digital Transformation," In *Harvard Business Review*. https://hbr.org/podcast/2019/12/how-one-ceo-successfully-led-a-digital-transformation

The Courage to Change

Considering the average tenure of a public company CEO is five years, it takes extraordinary courage to build a Forever Company.[6] But a change is possible if the will to change is strong enough. And circumstances sometimes compel the change. During the pandemic, companies made changes that otherwise would have taken years to complete. Retailers and grocers began using their physical stores as e-commerce fulfillment centers. Anheuser-Busch went from producing beer to producing hand sanitizer; Ford and GM used their manufacturing capability to create ventilators. Boeing delivered thousands of 3D-printed face shields, and Brooks Brothers made 150,000 masks per day.

These shifts in production and fulfillment were always options for these companies and illustrate my point. Companies can turn quickly in difficult circumstances. Circumstances might affect the decisions, but they don't make them. The capacity to change needs to be coupled with the will to change. Using the existing manufacturing capability to produce new products for new markets was always an option for Ford, GM, and Boeing. While I'm not advocating that Ford should go into the health care equipment business, I am illuminating they could. The decision to live is just that, a decision, not a circumstance. Companies are never victims of disruption; they are enablers of disruption.

 Truth Bomb: Companies are never victims of disruption; they are enablers of disruption.

Paradoxically, the question "Do you want to live?" can be coupled with the question, "Are you willing to die … at least a little bit?" Dying is risking. And to live requires risk. Walmart, Netflix, Adobe, Verizon, Shaw, PayPal, Apple, and Wolters Kluwer decided to live. And every other company can make the same decision.

---

[6] PricewaterhouseCoopers. 2019. "CEO Turnover at Record High; Successors Following Long Serving CEOs Struggling According to PwC's Strategy&Global Study," *PwC*. www.pwc.com/gx/en/news-room/press-releases/2019/ceo-turnover-record-high.html

Wrongly Confident

Companies don't make poor decisions; people do. Most often, the decision to do the same thing over and over again originates from intelligent people who have made so many good decisions that they have lost their ability to be humble. They don't think to ask, "Has this good decision gone bad?" Executives tend to stick with what has worked. It helps them feel confident. Their worldview is rarely challenged. Ironically, because they are often not reflective enough to ask the hard questions, take risks, and court failure, they come across as confident and visionary. According to Softbank Senior VP Ivo Rook, the danger is that executives can be too smart and "therefore sleepwalk yourself into becoming irrelevant over time."[7]

 Gold Nugget: You can actually be too smart and therefore sleepwalk yourself into becoming irrelevant over time.

The cliché, "always confident, sometimes right," often applies to corporate leaders who've been groomed to exude confidence. This creates a virtuous circle: when a leader projects confidence, people follow them, even if their choices are not optimum. If enough people provide muscle toward a vision, even if it's lackluster, the company will achieve a modicum of success—enough success for leaders to execute the same playbook.

If a company has been successful with its value proposition, it will see no need to change it. The market loves consistency of performance, but consistency is not reality, and reality finds a way. A hallmark of General Electric was its consistency of earnings. We now know that Neutron Jack (CEO Jack Welch) was tweaking earnings at GE Capital for years to get that consistency until the merry-go-round stopped.[8]

---

[7] I. Rook. November 26, 2018. "Former Senior Vice President, Sprint." Interview by Alan Amling.

[8] J.B. Stewart. 2017. "Did the Jack Welch Model Sow Seeds of G.E.'s Decline?" *The New York Times*, 2017/06/15/ 2017, Business, www.nytimes.com/2017/06/15/business/ge-jack-welch-immelt.html, NYTimes.com

Becoming a Forever Company requires that you keep your current business healthy while also creating new revenue and profit streams. The impetus for these new businesses typically has to come from within organizations. As one COO put it: "It's not about sharpening the knife, it's about creating a new knife. And the consultants with McKinsey & Company are not going to recommend that you create a new knife. They won't do it."

 Gold Nugget: It's not about sharpening the knife; it's about creating a new knife.

Consultants who want their clients to rehire them won't recommend switching knives. More importantly, there's no way an external force, like a consultant, can create lasting change within an organization. Instead of merely sharpening the existing one, the decision to create a new knife must originate internally; such decisions must be made for the right reasons. Like sobriety or weight loss, fundamental lifestyle changes can only be sustained if they are internally motivated; people want to do it for themselves and their reasons. The same is true for organizations. Organizations often stimulate change with flavor-of-the-month programs and innovation rhetoric that are not backed up by proportional changes in resource allocation and incentive systems. Change is hard and superficial motivations won't bridge the hard times that ensue. Mindsets must change before actions have a chance of succeeding.

A Forever Mindset: A Present Purpose

Walmart, and companies like it, are forever companies. Their leadership "thinks different," making their behavior unpredictable, unlike the companies who plan to do tomorrow precisely what they did today. Formulaic behavior is typical of aging leadership. Instead of playing the long game, they look to improve their financial wellbeing in the short run. The closer they are to retirement, the less likely they are to take risks for the long term. They think: why sacrifice near-term profit and put retirement funds at risk for a future payoff another leader will get credit for?[9]

On the other hand, age is irrelevant for senior teams who view themselves as stewards of a Forever Company, where profit is a means, not an end. A Forever Company is a mindset, an attitude that drives decisions that will enable the company to maintain its capacity for independent action into the future. To create that kind of legacy, a leader must engage its people in its larger purpose. They need to feel they are part of the company's story.

I fight to hold myself back from going on a rant when I hear someone say, "Business isn't personal." We've heard it enough to assume it's true. But, it isn't. Business is highly personal. Think about the last time you had a bad day at work. Did you really forget about it when you left the office? How did your day impact your friends and loved ones? You wouldn't dare tell someone who has lost their job that it's not personal. When companies refuse to engage in the future, they put the livelihoods of their employees at risk. And when they engage, their employees gain more than money. They gain a sense of purpose. Money helps you live, but it doesn't make life fulfilling. Meaningful work does, creating the feeling that you are part of a larger purpose and contributing to what matters in the long term.

 Truth Bomb: Business is highly personal.

A Forever Company creates opportunities for those within the company. Its leadership makes decisions that allow people to engage in a mission and stay employed for the long term. Day-to-day operational decisions are, of course, essential, as are improvements in efficiency or cutbacks, including layoffs. That's endemic to the work of business leadership.

---

[9] C. Adair. April 09, 2020. "Former Vice Chairman, BMO Capital Markets." Interview by Alan Amling.

But leaders who have their hand on the plow are also looking for fertile ground elsewhere.

In the digital economy, most companies will not stick with one line of business for 25 or 50 years as they did in the past. If they aspire to become a Forever Company, iterative learning must define them. A Forever Company is in a constant state of cultural and business process reinvention.

 Gold Nugget: A Forever Company is in a constant state of cultural and business process reinvention.

Organizational Velocity is the ability to absorb what's happening in the external environment, learn from it, and act accordingly. It's a mindset. It's a "lifestyle." It's embedded into the culture and the everyday decision-making process.

In the digital economy, it's much easier to process information than to act on it. It's the "acting upon it," however, that enables companies to learn quickly. And in turn, the acting informs the learning. The Forever Company culture supports failure, allowing young or new leaders to make decisions and fail. The opportunity—and the encouragement— to fail will help develop them into Fourth Industrial Revolution leaders. A company can absorb minor failures, which have a disproportionately positive impact on the decision maker. The knowledge gained from those early decisions, and getting a feeling for the process, will guide the leader when making decisions that are more significant.

People make decisions every day that can make the organization weaker or stronger over time. In my experience, it's rare that people don't care about their decision making or that they care only about themselves. More often, leaders don't realize the damage to their companies when their decisions simply maintain the status quo.

Is UPS a Forever Company?
The Story Is Still Being Written

Since its founding, UPS has innovated, adapted, and thrived. UPS would have been a minor historical footnote if its leadership hadn't effectively responded to its first technological disruption: the telephone. The messenger service was in a freefall.

UPS founder, Jim Casey, took stock of the assets at his disposal and focused on delivering packages from local merchants to homes. He and his partners continually improved delivery by consolidating packages through a hub-and-spoke network and adding new automation, such as conveyor belts. Over the next four decades, UPS expanded across the United States and experimented with delivery via air.

In 1975, UPS expanded services to Toronto and a year later to West Germany. UPS bled cash for many years in the international business, which would become a primary profit driver in the 2000s. In 1988, UPS responded to FedEx's threat by starting an airline from scratch; it was the fastest major airline startup in FAA history. These two bold moves (going international and starting an airline) established UPS as a Forever Company.

Its last bold move was to expand into the broader freight forwarding and distribution market in 1992, followed by a string of acquisitions in 2000 shortly after going public. Nonetheless, since going public, its decisions have been more measured, cautious. In 2001, UPS acquired Mail Boxes Etc. and Overnite Freight, and health care logistics company Marken in 2016. In 2019, the company launched the UPS Flight Forward drone airline. These were all solid incremental expansions. At the same time, the digital economy had taken root and was expanding exponentially.

You are in real-time on the field and only viewing what's immediately in front of you. When the company went public, I felt the change but couldn't fully appreciate the impact: when a "Forever Company" goes public, its metrics change. When UPS expanded internationally, it was still a private company, willing to suffer years of losses in the hopes of long-term gains. The metrics were "progress to profitability." Owners can withstand the near-term pain for long-term gain. Before it went public, UPS was a partnership owned by managers and managed by owners. We were incented for the longer haul.

While UPS has struggled as a public company, the UPS story is still being written. The new CEO has instituted bold moves that back up the "better, not bigger" and "sweat the assets" rhetoric. Streamlining decision making, spinning off the lower-margin trucking business, raising shipping rates, and slashing capital expenditures by $2 billion were hall-marks of her first full year at the helm. The UPS stock price rose more in Tomé's first six months as CEO than in the previous 20 years as a public company. Companies need to be successful in the Now before they can aspire to be Forever Companies, and UPS is doing that. However, the pattern of disruption over the last 20+ years indicates trouble ahead if the company's current trajectory does not change. When quarterly earnings calls begin to be dominated by words like "customer," "innovation," and "investment" compared to "results," "profits," and "earnings-per-share," you'll know UPS is on the way. It starts with a Forever Company mindset that permeates the organization.

In business, as in life, if there is no pain, there is no gain. Do you want to live? There will be some dying before the resurrection. But, to die is to live. It's the only way to thrive in a world of continuous disruption.

What?

Corporate longevity begins with answering a simple, profound question, "Do you want to live?"

So What?

Becoming a Forever Company is more often a choice than a circumstance. The "innovator's dilemma" is a dilemma precisely because choosing to live for the long term is the more difficult path. It requires certain sacrifices now for uncertain gains in the future. Without a core desire to be a Forever Company, change efforts will be more theater than substance.

Now What?

Organizational Velocity is a book for leaders that answered "yes" to "Do you want to live?" and are looking for insights that will help them build and sustain a Forever Company. It begins with the leader's mindset and permeates through the corporate ethos, structure, relationships, hiring practices, business processes, and inventive systems. Explore all these areas in the upcoming chapters.

CHAPTER 2

The Thinking Problem

The task is not so much to see what no one yet has seen, but to think what nobody yet has thought, about that which everybody sees.
—Arthur Schopenhauer

Organizational velocity (OV) leaders are great thinkers because they think about how and why they think what they think.

"This is all well and good, Alan, but how is this going to get us more packages or more money for the packages we send?"

The COO had asked the patently obvious question. And I knew the 3D Printing (also known as Additive Manufacturing or AM for short) initiative at UPS would do neither.

I had just spent a couple of years shepherding a novel concept to a fork in the road. An innovative UPS leader had researched the future of AM and its potential impact on the logistics business. He conceived the striking idea that UPS should pilot a small investment in an AM factory built within a UPS distribution center. As AM technology began to take hold, the futuristic thinking went, certain goods would be produced more frequently in lower quantities, closer to the point of consumption. UPS already had a global footprint, so similar factories could be stamped out anywhere in the world.

The beauty of AM, of course, is that there is no product mold. By eliminating the significant up-front investment on a mold, the need to sell thousands of the products merely to breakeven also goes away. Production is quick and low cost for limited quantities. A future of products tailored to individuals, where demand is created before supply, comes into view: a vision, consequently, that portends less need for storage and fewer shipments. UPS-ers used to say that we have nothing to worry about until "Beam me up Scotty" becomes a reality. I realized that time was fast approaching. UPS could either be a part of the trend—or its victim.

I was invited to join the initiative, and soon our partner, Fast Radius, established their first AM "Micro-factory" at UPS's national air hub. I became the face of AM at UPS and was energized about the possibilities.

After several years of intense learning, we had to decide: either to lean into AM or refocus on other initiatives. While AM had advanced, it was far from mature. For most applications, it was still too slow and too expensive. I wanted to lean in. I put together documents, customer videos, and presentations to educate the management team, eventually asking for a modest investment. UPS could continue to be an arms merchant to the world, I argued, serving all AM companies with our logistics and package delivery services, or we could move upstream. We could become an on-demand manufacturer, create new manufacturing revenue streams with our customers, and take a leadership role in the emerging digital supply chain.

The CEO and CTO (chief transformation officer) seemed genuinely excited about the potential of AM at UPS. Everyone else—the intelligent, experienced executive team with tremendous day-to-day demands— hated it. "Come back when AM is 'real,'" was a common refrain, a backhanded acknowledgment that AM was on its way to becoming accretive to profits but still too risky an endeavor. Tolerance for uncertainty in a company known for efficiency was not high.

The COO's hardball question mirrored this mindset. I hoped my answer might open the door to another way of thinking.

"It won't," I replied. "If that's what you want out of this investment, UPS should not invest in it. Only invest in it if you want to create new revenue streams with our customers and to become a leader in this emerging digital supply chain."

This venture into AM was not part of the UPS mindset—efficiency was. At this moment, I could empathize with how Kodak's Steve Sasson, the inventor of digital photography, may have felt when he positioned a technology with the potential to disrupt his company's core business. Film photography was the core business; digital photography was a hobby. Two-and-a-half Kodak CEOs looked brilliant, focusing on their highly profitable core business until the market turned in 1992, leading to a painful 20-year slide to bankruptcy.

This was a mindset problem. Narrowly defining its industry was a classic case of what Theodore Levitt called "marketing myopia."[1] Kodak thought it was in the film business, not in the business of capturing and storing memories. Likewise, Blockbuster was in the video rental business, Borden was in the dairy business, and UPS was in the package delivery business. John Casesa, a former Ford executive, lamented how the company could not understand how Uber's brief but expansive brand message, "moving people," would be important.[2] It was the breakaway antithesis of marketing myopia.

Changing your mindset is a choice incumbents make when they refuse to accept what their environmental observations are telling them. While I don't have the inside story on Marriott and Hilton, I am confident they heard about Airbnb in 2008. As late as 2015, Chris Nasetta, the CEO of Hilton Worldwide, stated, "I do not believe—strongly do not believe— they (Airbnb) are a major threat to the core value proposition we have."[3] Today Hilton still has a viable business, but Airbnb had 247 million guest arrivals in 2019 and a market value more than Hilton and Marriott combined.[4] Not a threat? In 2019, Marriott finally accepted what the market had been telling them and launched a home rental business.[5]

In chapter 1, I made the case that the Fourth Industrial Revolution is different from previous revolutions.[6] Artificial Intelligence (AI), machine

---

[1] T. Levitt. 1960. "Marketing Myopia," *Harvard Business Review* 38, no. 4.

[2] J. Casesa. January 11, 2019. "Senior Managing Director at Guggenheim Partners and former Group Vice President, Ford Motor Company." Interview by Alan Amling.

[3] B. Bryan. October 29, 2015. "Hilton CEO: Airbnb Doesn't Scare Us—Here's Why," *Business Insider*, www.businessinsider.com/hilton-ceo-airbnb-competition-2015-10

[4] "Airbnb's IPO: 6 Key Things to Know," *Fortune*, https://fortune.com/2020/12/09/airbnb-ipo-share-price-covid-revenue-profit-2020-brian-chesky-abnb-nasdaq// (accessed December 09, 2020).

[5] N. El-Bawab. April 29, 2019. "Marriott Plans to Launch Home-Rental Market Platform that Would Compete with Airbnb, Report Says," In *CNBC*, www.cnbc.com/2019/04/29/marriott-to-launch-home-rental-platform-to-compete-with-airbnb-report.html

[6] K. Schwab. 2017. *The Fourth Industrial Revolution*. Currency.

learning, Internet of Things, robotics, and AM, among other technologies, are fusing our digital and physical worlds. These digital threats
pose risks to those who aspire to lead their companies forward in the
21st century.[7] The biggest threat to most incumbent businesses, however,
is not disruptive technological innovation. The problem of disruptive
technology is largely a fixable problem solved with attention, creativity,
and capital. The core issue, and deeper problem, is an entrenched way of
thinking that stubbornly persists even after a couple of decades of digital
disruption, unlimited books and conferences on the subject, and minions
of consultants waving the revolutionary flag.

 Gold Nugget: Technology is largely a fixable problem solved
with attention, creativity, and capital.

Wait for It. Wait for It. Wow, That Was Fast!

Companies are often taken by surprise by the rapid ascension of an
upstart competitor. Executives can be lulled to sleep by an unimpressive
new offering at the low end of the market. They may see improvement in
the product over time but misjudge the increasing pace of those changes.
They are thinking linearly, while the change in the digital economy is
often exponential. The oft-told story of the lily pad that grows exponentially to cover the entire pond in three years is applicable here (i.e., after
one month, there will be two lily pads, after two months, there will be

---

[7] In this book, I am addressing the specific threat of disruptive innovation only,
where new competitors target non-consumption at the low end of the market.
Incumbent organizations tend to focus primarily on higher margin products,
serving customers farther upstream, what is called "sustaining innovation." But
they often ignore the bottom of the market at their peril, given today's learning and connecting technologies. Start-ups often take the low ground first and
then improve the quality of their products, eventually surpassing the incumbent.
Tesla, the electric car company started by Elon Musk, would not be considered
an example of disruptive innovation in the automotive space, but it may be in
battery storage. Tesla attacked the high end of the market and went directly after
the big car companies.

four, etc.). If asked when the pond would be half-filled with lily pads, the tendency would be to predict half the time or 18 months. In fact, it would take until month 35.[8] Progress in the early days was almost imperceptibly slow, but it wasn't invisible. Toward the end of the cycle, it appears the lily pads came out of nowhere.

We're seeing this phenomenon now with technologies like blockchain, AM, and new AI-driven business models in incubators across the country. But it's not enough to see the change; firms have to accept that the change could impact their business and allocate current resources to deploy against what may be a threat ... or not. While it's easy to disparage those that didn't move to blunt a disruptive force, would you want to be the one convincing managers to forgo investment in profits today for uncertain profits tomorrow?

Ric Fulop, Founder and CEO of Desktop Metal, one of the fastest-growing "unicorns" in U.S. history, is living through this evolution in the AM industry.

"The world of technology is replete with examples where humans overestimate the short term and underestimate the long term," said Rick, "If you asked somebody in the 1970s about computing which was invented in the 50s, they would think computers are reserved for the largest corporations to do their work. Meanwhile, you had a personal computer developing which nobody took seriously that made it affordable for everybody to get it."[9]

Today the power of computing is not only in our homes, but also in our hands. There are more than 5 billion people with mobile devices.[10] But initially, like the lily pads, progress was slow. A lot of naysayers looked brilliant during that time, until they didn't. While computing

---

[8] J. Becher. 2016. "Lily Pads and Exponential Thinking," *Manage By Walking Around.* https://jonathanbecher.com/2016/01/31/lily-pads-and-exponential-thinking/

[9] R. Fulop. October 05, 2020. "Founder & CEO, Desktop Metal." Interview by Alan Amling.

[10] L. Silver. February 05, 2019. "Smartphone Ownership Is Growing Rapidly Around the World, But Not Always Equally" *Pew Research Center's Global Attitudes Project.* www.pewresearch.org/global/2019/02/05/smartphone-ownership-is-growing-rapidly-around-the-world-but-not-always-equally/2019

was invented in the 50s, it didn't make it into our homes until the 80s. In the 80s, cell phones were high-cost bricks. By 2015, the Apple Watch had the computing power of two Cray supercomputers from 1985. From the 80s to the current day, the pace of change has only accelerated. The "computing pond" is not yet half-full.

 Truth Bomb: Humans overestimate the short term and underestimate the long term.

What do you think of AM today, if you think about it at all? Unlike computers, AM has not yet had its breakout moment. While the technology was invented in the 80s, the cost, quality, and material selection are still not competitive with existing manufacturing techniques for most applications. It's easier and a lot less mentally taxing to ignore AM or make it a hobby if you're in manufacturing. However, if you knew for sure that AM would allow you to manufacture customized products at a comparable cost and quality to current mass manufacturing techniques, what would you do differently? If you knew for sure in 1985 that 30 years later, you would have more computing power for less money on your wrist, what would you have done differently? The tea leaves in the market are there to read if we're open and prepared to do so. It's not a technology problem; it's a thinking problem.

 Truth Bomb: It's not a technology problem; it's a thinking problem.

Scholars C. K. Prahalad and Richard Bettis tackled the issue of entrenched mindsets in their theory of dominant logic.[11] Essentially, companies get fixed on what rings the cash register (i.e., their dominant logic), and it's difficult for them to conceptualize other ways to earn revenue. The force of dominant logic can be devastating. Nucor's mini-mill technology disrupted US Steel decades ago, but US Steel didn't invest in

---

[11] C.K. Prahalad and R.A. Bettis. 1986. "The Dominant Logic: A New Linkage Between Diversity and Performance," *Strategic Management Journal* 7, no. 6, pp. 485–501.

mini-mills until October of 2019. In February 2020, Nucor still held a market value nearly ten times higher than US Steel. Even more striking is Macy's slow response to e-commerce; as of June 2021, their $5.5 billion market cap is not even 1 percent of Amazon's market value. It wasn't until recently that a Macy's executive declared, "We found that technology is going to start to play a much bigger role in our future than it has in the past."[12] No kidding!

Disruption is inevitable, but the effects of disruption are not. If a leader of an incumbent organization aspires to live on in the Fourth Industrial Revolution, the future starts with thinking differently. No longer can leaders optimize their existing competitive advantage (same revenue stream, same customer) only. Legacy companies must also embrace what is called "persistent advantage"[13,14], i.e., innovating continually with technology to create new capabilities and revenue streams.

 Gold Nugget: Disruption is inevitable, but the effects of disruption are not.

From Chess to Mixed Martial Arts

In established companies, improving efficiencies is essential to sustaining innovation.[15] I'm certainly not arguing for inefficiency. The danger is when organizations become so good at incremental improvements that

---

[12] R. Habersham. February 23, 2020. "Macy's Tech Hub Brings Hundreds of Jobs to Midtown, Could Help Reinvigorate Company," *The Atlanta Journal-Constitution.* www.ajc.com/news/local/macy-tech-hub-midtown-could-help-reinvigorate-company/u3zkRGAPuiaytXb8rg2znL/

[13] L.A. Thomas. 1995. "Brand Capital and Incumbent Firms' Positions in Evolving Markets," *The Review of Economics and Statistics,* pp. 522–534. Thomas mentioned "persistent advantage" once, but he did not define the term.

[14] W. Darity, J. Dietrich, and D.K. Guilkey. 2001. "Persistent Advantage or Disadvantage?: Evidence in Support of the Intergenerational Drag Hypothesis," *American Journal of Economics and Sociology* 60, no. 2, pp. 435–470. Darity and Dietrich used "persistent advantage" in their title, but not in the text.

[15] I credit much of my thinking on sustaining innovation to Clayton Christensen, who coined sustaining and disruptive innovation in *The Innovator's Dilemma* (1997).

they become deadly efficient sharpening their knives while not creating new knives.

Sam Walton had the fresh idea that instead of maximizing profitability, Walmart would focus on volume, making a little less on each item sold, but selling more items. Walmart built a juggernaut on everyday low prices. Walmart could have continued to squeeze more efficiencies out of the supply chain. Instead, while Walmart was still the envy of the physical retail world, it launched a digital strategy that stays true to its core value of everyday low prices while also expanding to those who want to buy online and pick up in-store. While Amazon puts up more and more distribution centers, Walmart already has over 10,000 distribution centers across the world in the form of stores.

Walmart asked the disruptive question, "How can we use the store as a distribution center to deliver locally? How can we take what's good about the model, extend it into this new world, and create value for customers that wasn't there before?"

That's turning the efficiency mindset on its head. The endless pursuit of efficiency is, first and foremost, an entrenched belief system about the math of business. The efficiency mindset is baked in early on in the executive training regimen. If tomorrow were 1990, the product that business schools turn out year after year would still be highly coveted. The MBA degree is still a rite of passage for entering senior management ranks in many incumbent organizations. Most MBA programs teach management more as a science than as a profession by professors who know the path but have seldom walked it. The curriculum focuses on discrete elements of the business (operations, marketing, finance, IT systems, supply chain, management, etc.) and equips students with formulas to solve historical problems. Students debate packaged case studies about past successes and failures. By the time these studies run the gauntlet of peer review, they are sometimes five years old or more. This kind of rigorous training—and thus approach to thinking about business problems—assumes a flat world. A world that can be mapped and organized, and graphed. A world before 1995, when Netscape ripped the curtain off the existing world order, giving everyone low-cost access to limitless information at their fingertips.

The modern MBA trains students to play chess, a sophisticated game of moves and countermoves. In chess, there are only two opponents and 64 squares. Each player has 16 pieces and the rules for winning are clear: checkmate. The game is a perfect metaphor for the skills needed for sustaining innovation. Good chess players anticipate scenarios and plan their moves far in advance. However, the digital economy demands different thinking, more like how an MMA (mixed martial arts) fighter acts and reacts. As with chess, he or she studies an opponent's strengths and weaknesses, watches film, and plans for the match. But once the bell rings and the fighters touch gloves, the match takes on an unpredictable narrative. As boxer Mike Tyson famously quipped, "Everyone has a plan until they get punched in the mouth."[16]

 Gold Nugget: The digital economy requires a different kind of thinking, more like MMA fighters than Chess Masters.

MMA fighting is all about adapting quickly to reactions. Unlike chess, MMA is lightning fast and unpredictable. An MMA fight is asynchronous, fluid, and full of surprises. The best fighters adapt quickly and learn on the fly, making continual adjustments to their opponent's moves as the fight ensues. The speed and stakes of MMA are not that of chess. No math can plan for five periods of a championship MMA. There's no algorithm (at least not yet) that can model the unpredictability of MMA.

The chess mindset works beautifully for sustaining innovations. It's invaluable for optimizing the business. While incumbent organizations continue to need chess players, the relentless pursuit of optimization creates inevitable growth risk over time. One executive said to me, "When you are so entrenched in your existing business, it's difficult to know what is actually transformational and where you should invest outside of just optimizing." Some have argued for hiring ambidextrous managers who

[16] M. Berardino. November 09, 2012. "Mike Tyson Explains One of his Most Famous Quotes," *Sun-Sentinel.com*. www.sun-sentinel.com/sports/fl-xpm-2012-11-09-sfl-mike-tyson-explains-one-of-his-most-famous-quotes-20121109-story.html

can manage processes while also fostering innovation.[17] David Kidder, the author of *New to Big*, said it this way: "The role of creating growth is the opposite of operating, which means future CEOs are going to be ambidextrous leaders. They're going to be great investors and great optimizers."[18] But, most managers today are either one or the other.

 Truth Bomb: The role of creating growth is the opposite of operating.

An MMA fighter has a unique mindset and thought process, able to adapt to every move. Fighters figure out how to solve problems (fists, headbutts, kicks, takedowns, and chokeholds) as they flash in real-time.

Fresh out of college, my son landed his first job at an AM startup company. His first assignment was to tinker with some first-generation 3D printers and get them to work. "You are not going to believe this," he said. "None of these machines have user manuals."

"You've been given a great gift," I said, "the gift of figuring it out." The mindset of figuring it out and learning from your mistakes is much different from the planning mindset, which is locked into processes for calculating marginal costs and increasing operational efficiencies. A company that hires only MBAs can end up with teams who all think the same way, equipped to create more processes that fortify the bureaucracy.

Faux Behavior

"If we don't please investors today, there won't be a tomorrow."

This is the dominant default mindset of most public companies. One CEO, whom I interviewed, put it frankly, "There is no long term without the short term." To assuage their anxiety about innovation, executives will dabble in innovation initiatives, but when the portfolio isn't performing well (and the innovation portfolios rarely perform as the pro forma

---

[17] M.L. Tushman and C.A. O'Reilly III. 1996. "Ambidextrous Organizations: Managing Evolutionary and Revolutionary Change," *California management Review* 38, no. 4.

[18] D. Kidder. February 21, 2019. "CEO, Bionic." Interview by Alan Amling.

gloriously promises), the reptilian side of their brain takes over, "We're not going to make our numbers. Let's focus on the core and keep moving forward." A sense of resignation follows, "That's just the way it is; you can't fight it."

A publicly traded consumer goods company recently recruited a technology executive to build its data science infrastructure. The company's leadership team had realized their customers had gained a much better command of their data, which diminished the traditional value of the company brands. Ten years behind in their data science capabilities, they needed to catch up quickly. The new Lead Data Scientist immediately recruited a team to work across the enterprise to create a data-centered model.

When the leader returned with a plan to accelerate the company's data capabilities, management punched him in the face with the status quo. "We'll give you 10 percent of what you asked for. Prove that you can get a return on that 10 percent, and we'll give you more." This is a typical, pragmatic response from an established company dealing with the demands of existing customers, competitors, and shareholders. The problem with this non-action is as fundamental as the business itself. All companies make trade-offs between time, cost, and scope. For example, if you increase the scope, you must also increase time or cost. In this case, the scope was enormous and the time was short. In this context, the "10 percent" answer created an exercise in futility. Management made the press-release statement that they wanted to be data-driven, but their actions did not back it up. Would they have made the same decision if data science was seen as a growth center rather than a cost center?

Changing actions without first changing the leaders' shortsighted mindset is futile because the end of the quarter is never more than three months away. Time is always short. The math that leaders use to report to the board and investors is simple. And irrefutable. Faced with the numbers, the senior team reveals their traditional mindset; new initiatives are shoved underwater. Not surprisingly, a recent downturn of this company's stock

---

Gold Nugget: Changing actions without first changing the leaders' mindset is futile because the end of the quarter is never more than three months away.

price was credited in part to its lack of data infrastructure. This issue, however, is not an isolated illness; it's an epidemic.

The lack of data infrastructure was not the only root cause of the value destruction of the firm's brands. Wall Street analysts blamed the company's belt-tightening strategy that went too far (coupled with declining sales in its traditional brands). Nonetheless, a data-centric business model is endemic to thriving in the Fourth Industrial Revolution.[19]

This business model needs to be driven by a corresponding mindset. Research published by MIT in 2020 showed that just 12 percent of respondents strongly agreed that their leaders have the right mindsets to lead them forward. While 82 percent believe that leaders need to be digitally savvy, less than 10 percent strongly agreed that their organization has leaders with the right skills to thrive in the digital economy.[20]

Often, an organization's response to an imminent threat or even opportunity is not driven by a change in the leadership's belief system. Executive FOMO (Fear of Missing Out) may cause them to act in a way that seems strategically innovative. Much of this is a form of what has been called innovation theater. For example, companies create "innovation" teams that never incubate long enough to innovate and are quietly disbanded when it's time to cinch up the belt. Lucky executives are whisked off to cutting-edge strategy conferences and return trumpeting the language of "value innovation" or whatever is the latest mantra.[21] Actions that arise from innovation theater are superficial. Leadership behavior is not supported by a change in worldview. Executives return from their boondoggle refreshed, motivated, armed with new metrics; they feign change, yet everything for which they are accountable never changes. The coup de grâce is when the company hires a world-class

[19] A. Gasparro. February 21, 2019. "Kraft Heinz Divulges SEC Investigation, Swings to Loss—WSJ," *The Wall Street Journal.* www.wsj.com/articles/kraft-heinz-discloses-sec-probe-misses-earnings-forecasts-11550789493

[20] D. Ready, C. Cohen, D. Kiron, and B. Pring. 2020. "The New Leadership Playbook for the Digital Age," *MIT Sloan Management Review.*

[21] S. Blank. 2019. "Why Companies Do 'Innovation Theater' Instead of Actual Innovation," *Harvard Business Review,* https://hbr.org/2019/10/why-companies-do-innovation-theater-instead-of-actual-innovation

consulting firm to interview all the employees, who already had the innovative ideas in the first place, and drafts a strategic innovation plan that is never implemented.

A recent Accenture survey illuminates the problem: while most companies demonstrate a strong commitment to innovation, few are actually innovating. According to the survey, 82 percent of organizations run innovation exactly the same way they run regular operations, with an overriding commitment to the status quo. The result is that 72 percent admit they missed a crucial growth opportunity.[22]

For many leaders, innovation is merely theater. It's faux. It's jejune. Corporate actions will never change until the belief system is altered.

The Consensus Mindset

At UPS, I was tasked with making the case to the CEO and the executive team for a new business venture in reverse logistics, a growing area in the expanding world of e-commerce. The project aimed to make UPS a provider of systemic reverse logistics solutions instead of returns transportation only. The results would be two-fold: economic and environmental sustainability for both UPS and our customers. My direct managers were all in the room. I had alerted them to how I planned to move the new initiative through the process. This meeting was not a deep dive into the proposal. It was simply a pre-meeting to set the stage for the full proposal.

It worked. The CEO was convinced that UPS had to move forward and asked point-blank, "So what is the proposal, exactly?" He felt a sense of urgency—and wanted to dig into the details. Think for a moment about what you might do in this situation. The direct manager wanted consensus for the proposal before sharing it with the CEO, who was now in front of me asking for it. Despite the dagger eyes from my management team, I dug in; and planted the right seed in the wrong soil! My managers had agreed to what was in the proposal but were unwilling

---

[22] "Three Years Later, U.S. Companies Continue to Struggle With Innovation, Accenture Survey Reveals," *Newsroom*. www./news/three-years-later-us-companies-continue-to-struggle-with-innovation-accenture-survey-reveals.htm (accessed March 21, 2016).

to take the risk of acting on it without previous consensus from the leadership team. I overstepped my bounds, again, and a new leader was tapped for the project. Over the next two years, she trudged through a series of additional presentations and proposals before leaving the company. The project—which I figured cost UPS over a million dollars—was shelved after keeping it on life support for several years. The issue is not whether the innovation was right. That was unknowable. However, the idea could have been tested five years earlier for a fraction of the cost to determine if it was viable. The organization's consensus mindset was not ready for that.

Consensus thinking may be the number one killer of innovative thinking in incumbent organizations. Dr. Joe Astrachan, Emeritus Professor of Management at Kennesaw State University, saw groupthink smother innovation in several boards he chaired. He says consensus is not agreement; it's not even a solution everyone thinks they can live with. Consensus is when a group talks and talks until the person with the most power in the room says, "I think we have a consensus, and it is x." If there is any lingering disagreement, talking continues, and the process repeats until no one voices disagreement.[23] An Amazon executive I spoke with put it this way, "You put all these people together and end up getting a negotiated outcome that doesn't actually appease anyone. So, you have to ask what value are you ever really creating by aligning across the organization?"

> ☀ Truth Bomb: Consensus is when a group talks and talks and the person with the most power in the room says, "I think we have a consensus, and it is x."

The consensus mindset strives to avoid the kind of open conflict that might lead to new discoveries. A lack of open conflict characterizes political systems. In the absence of an all-powerful leader, political systems cannot innovate. People are afraid to risk saying something. Reaching

---

[23] J. Astrachan. May 25, 2020. "Professor Universitat Witten/Herdecke, Family Business Fellow, Cornell Johnson Graduate School of Management, Board of Directors for 9 companies." Interview by Alan Amling.

consensus on a purportedly innovative idea is the surest sign that the idea is not innovative. And if the loudest voice in the room (the archetypical Alpha Dog) drives decision making, then the risk just increased. George Manners, a former professor, inventor, and Director at James River, sums it up. "In the absence of data, bullies and bullshitters always win."[24] The data exists somewhere, of course, but it's held hostage in siloes and isn't readily available or transparent to the decision makers.

 Truth Bomb: In the absence of data, bullies and bullshitters always win.

The consensus mindset can also be described as a high-cost safety net. When consensus is reached, responsibility is diffused. Large bets need broad support. But when a firm truly understands the downside of consensus, they move forward with small risks that are not hampered by the consensus process before the commercial truth is revealed.

Uncertainty Is an Unlikely Friend

There's a chasm of difference between risk and uncertainty. Risk can be mitigated with analysis. With risk comes a known range of outcomes that can be quantified using probabilities.[25] There is no data to mitigate uncertainty fully; the threat has yet to materialize. Apple was not even on Nokia's list of competitors one year before the iPhone launched and began to erode Nokia's position in the market.[26]

Uncertainty may be the most accurate word to describe both the mood and context of the Fourth Industrial Revolution. If the most crucial

---

[24] G.E. Manners, Jr and R.T. Barth. 1978. "Organizational Climate Factors and the Evaluation of Technical Ideas," *R&D Management* 8, no. 3.

[25] D. Teece, M. Peteraf, and S. Leih. 2016. "Dynamic Capabilities and Organizational Agility: Risk, Uncertainty, and Strategy in the Innovation Economy," *California Management Review* 58, no. 4.

[26] R.G. McGrath. 2010. "Business Models: A Discovery Driven Approach," *Long Range Planning* 43, no. 2–3.

information for an incumbent company's future is the data that has not yet been created, senior management must grasp the significant difference between risk and uncertainty. An organization adapts and moves its way to the future in response to observed human behavior, which also helps organizations predict human behavior. Uncertainty makes this impossible. This is where leaders of incumbent organizations falter: action must be taken before outcomes are known.

 Truth Bomb: Action must be taken before outcomes are known.

However, today's managers appear weak if they cannot confidently predict the future. This leads to a kind of uncertainty-driven dishonesty, especially when it's combined with the allure of improving efficiency and profitability. If I, as a manager, am not introducing anything new, then I'm taking out of the equation the most significant source of uncertainty. If I'm not innovating and piloting new initiatives, I'm only sharpening the blade; every decision is about marginal cost. If everything is a marginal cost, then short-term profitability will improve. When metrics are tied to capital efficiency measures, the safest play is to improve what I have. Iconic brands often rely on their historical success and are slow to respond to the shifting tastes of the consumer. A good example is the dairy industry, where brands like Borden's and Dean's never responded effectively to trends of soymilk and other alternatives, resulting in bankruptcy. Kraft relied on zero-based budgeting for years, starving its brands of innovation while boosting profits through cost cutting. Without reinvesting in innovation (and self-disruption is seen as an enormous risk), profits do not ensure survival.

Measures Matter

If that's how managers are evaluated, they can't take all the blame. They simply mirror the systemic worldview of the leaders at the top of the house, including the board of directors. In general, established firms tend to favor capital allocation metrics like return on invested capital (ROIC) and earnings before interest, tax, depreciation, and amortization

(EBITDA). A COO said in an interview, "We do a good bit of marginal analysis in [our firm], and most people … can do a 15-year net present value in their head darn near off of EBITDA. We're good with math. And so, we want to make sure that we're kind of seeing the signs of the benefits materialize to give us confidence that we keep going so we don't just run down an alley for two or three years."

The issue is not about running down an alley with bad math. The problem is the deep-rutted thinking that there is only one kind of math tied to short-term profitability. Another recent conversation with an executive captures the essence of the mindset problem: "This is where I struggle," he said, "because many of the companies that people say are successful, how do we measure those companies? So, Uber, okay, successful company, by what standard? From a profitability standard? I don't think so. They don't make any money."

There is not one kind of business math that fits all. Newer firms tend to favor metrics that are aligned with growth, not profitability. That doesn't mean that established enterprises can't become growth companies (and capital markets love growth companies!). Bill Gates grew Microsoft into a $600B powerhouse over his 25 years. Over the next 14 years, the incremental strategies of Steve Ballmer cut the company's value in half. Enter Satya Nadella, a longtime insider who reinvigorated Microsoft with a completely different mindset. He recaptured Microsoft's growth company status and supercharged the company's value over 430 percent to $1.3T by the 6th anniversary of his appointment as CEO.

Executives need to be comfortable being uncomfortable. The conversation has shifted from managing ambiguities to developing a strategy at the edge of being wrong. The Overton Window shown in Figure 2.1 can provide a framework to think about the aggressiveness and timing of proposed actions.[27]

Joseph Overton developed the framework to evaluate a range of ideas that may gain acceptance given the state of public opinion. The window ranges from unthinkable to popular, with gradations of radical, acceptable, and sensible until it becomes policy. In Figure 2.1, the Overton Window

---

[27] J. Lehman. 2014. "A Brief Explanation of the Overton Window," *Mackinac Center for Public Policy.*

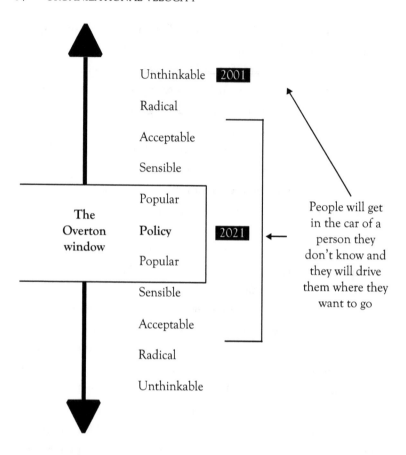

Figure 2.1 Overton's window

is applied to the proposition, "People will get into the car of a person they don't know who will drive them where they want to go." In a business context, multiple indicators will tell whether an action is right in time. For example, broadband adoption was an indicator of the viability of the Netflix move to streaming. A year earlier and their offering would likely have fallen flat. OV leaders need to live on the edge between radical and acceptable, leveraging real-time information from the external environment.

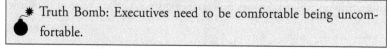

Truth Bomb: Executives need to be comfortable being uncomfortable.

For those not comfortable being uncomfortable, there is hope. It's a learned behavior and can be developed. Those public speakers that make speeches look effortless have put in hundreds of hours of work to make it look that way. At the fast-growing e-commerce company Shopify, employees will occasionally shift their mouse to their non-dominant hand to remind them not to be complacent.

Offense Is the New Defense

At the end of World War II, the United States captured several German generals, and some of the U.S. military's current strategy can be traced to interviews with those German generals. One of them was Hermann Balck, who led the 11th Panzer Division. Balck was known for nearly wiping out the Soviet Fifth Tank Army in a few weeks, even though he was outnumbered in infantry 11 to 1 and tanks by 7 to 1.[28] When asked how he succeeded, he said, "Go on offense. We never relented. We attack, attack, attack, attack, attack."

He explained that people have the misperception that it's safer to play defense than go on offense. They mistakenly think there will be more casualties going on the attack than trying to defend. There's nothing more immobilizing for established firms than the frightening uncertainty of going on offense. As businesses get bigger and bigger, they create processes to control their "bigness." They talk about sustainable competitive advantage and "creating moats" around their offerings through cost leadership or differentiation. Today, however, competing firms can cross those moats with increasing ease. Digital conglomerates like Amazon, Alibaba, Google, and Apple are leveraging Industry 4.0 technologies and customer-centric business models to penetrate multiple industries simultaneously. Today's leaders must practice second-order thinking pushing the envelope by asking, "And then what?"

> Gold Nugget: Companies make the mistake of thinking that there will be more casualties going on the attack than trying to defend.

---

[28] H. Balck. 2015. *Order in Chaos: The Memoirs of General of Panzer Troops Hermann Balck.* University Press of Kentucky.

Whenever one of UPS's 500,000-square-foot distribution centers was close to running out of capacity, a business case to build a new one was developed. However, before the senior team gave the green light to put up the building, UPS typically required at least half of the space to be pre-sold to clients. This invariably slowed down construction, which took about six months. During the same time, retailer Amazon was standing up the same-sized facility every month. We were getting lapped six times over, but there was no sense of urgency. No one said, "We need to move faster, or we'll be in trouble." Our burning question was, "What will this project do to our return on invested capital?" Our traditional competitors were using similar metrics, but Amazon was not. "Defending our moat" against traditional competitors using similar metrics opened the door to a new competitor that focused on receivers, not shippers. Amazon now has over 260 Distributions Centers and 450 Delivery Stations enabling short-zone same-day and next-day deliveries and turning the traditional hub-and-spoke delivery model on its head.[29] Playing not to lose is the surest way to lose.

 Truth Bomb: Playing not to lose is the surest way to lose.

When companies focus solely on a handful of tried-and-true formulas, they die a death by a thousand cuts, so small they are nearly imperceptible. Innovative companies eat away at the edges, stealing tiny slices of their value proposition. I started at UPS corporate as a competitive analyst. I spent my early years grinding through FedEx data, ripping apart their financial reports, and tracking the package vehicles leaving their facilities. FedEx made UPS a better company. When I moved to corporate strategy, I never laid awake at night worrying about FedEx. I knew that if FedEx invested a dollar in logistics, they had to make a dollar in logistics. Amazon, however, was a completely different animal (as were Walmart, Target, Alibaba, etc.). Amazon can invest a dollar in logistics and never have to make a dollar from logistics. It seems so obvious now. As recently as a decade ago, it wasn't.

The defensive mindset at the top trickles down to managers. They play "good soldier" and go on defense. A good soldier knows the processes

---

[29] "Amazon Distribution Network Strategy | MWPVL International," https://mwpvl.com/html/amazon_com.html (accessed September 2021).

inside and out and is mission-critical when the market is stable. When the market is churning, as it is today, a different kind of soldier is also needed, one who is trained to go on the offensive; who is comfortable with being uncomfortable. The ability to grow as an incumbent company in an uncertain world requires going on the offensive. The trick is to use existing resources to take the next step—to "discover growth." Moving into uncertainty demands being uncomfortable.[30]

Bionic CEO David Kidder recently said to me, "When you're going to the unknowable, you're going from planning to discovery. You don't plan the future; you discover growth in the future. When you're going for growth, the mindset of an investor is the opposite of an operator. It's a creator [mindset]."

 Gold Nugget: You don't plan the future; you discover growth in the future.

A creator can only be on offense because there is nothing yet to defend (or measure); it doesn't exist, so its data has not yet been created. The only way to protect against the relentless attack of more nimble learning-and-connecting companies is to go on offense. Offense is the best defense. Several military theories that support this come from John Boyd, whom I introduced earlier. Boyd's theories influenced everything from the design of the F16 to the US assault strategies in Iraq.[31] Still, he's best known for his "OODA Loop," which stands for observation, orientation, decision, and action cycles. It's a conceptual model built around going on offense while adapting to changing conditions. Boyd believed that only open systems could adapt adequately to change. This was demonstrated by his loop-back model that increases a leader's ability to make decisions faster than the adversary because real-time information is leveraged.[32]

[30] D. Kidder and C. Wallace. 2019. *New to Big: How Companies Can Create Like Entrepreneurs, Invest Like VCs, and Install a Permanent Operating System for Growth.* Currency.

[31] J. Fallows. 2014. "John Boyd, From US News," *The Atlantic.* www.theatlantic .com/national/archive/2014/03/john-boyd-from-em-us-news-em/284223/

[32] J. Boyd. 2018. *A Discourse on Winning and Losing,* Vol. 13. Air University Press.

Gold Nugget: Offense is the best defense.

Boyd's OODA Loop is not a "how-to" guide; it's a way of thinking based on centuries of military and academic theory, science, and experience. The series of feedback loops don't create set answers as to the future of the company. The loop of current data—continuously monitored, analyzed, and assimilated—creates a system that continually adapts to the changing reality. It's constantly being "refreshed." A leader's mental patterns should be fluid, based on the business context and what's happening "on the ground."

Offense is, first of all, a mindset.

This mindset is prominent in Jeff Bezos' 2016 letter to Amazon shareholders, which highlighted not only making "high-quality" decisions but "high-velocity" decisions. The two go hand in hand. "Most decisions," writes Bezos, "should probably be made with somewhere around 70 percent of the information you wish you had. If you wait for 90 percent, in most cases you're probably slow." Choosing not to move forward fast comes at a price; that is, "if you're good at course correcting," Bezos continued, "being wrong may be less costly than you think, whereas being slow is going to be expensive for sure."[33] Moving fast involves failure, for which the "course correction" compensates so you can learn fast from your failures. If you're not course correcting and thus learning about what's not working well, moving fast is simply a waste of resources.

Slow Is a Choice

UPS ultimately made the investment in AM, but the resources and support didn't follow. The epilogue does not condemn the executives who wanted to do the right thing. They acted with integrity and confidence within the parameters of the mindset that governed their careers.

I was perhaps the guiltiest of all in terms of a fixed mindset. It was my job to champion AM, like thousands of leaders who fight every day for

---

[33] J. Bezos. 2017. "Amazon 2016 Letter to Shareholders," *Exhibit 99.1*. www.sec.gov/Archives/edgar/data/1018724/000119312517120198/d373368dex991.htm

the projects on which their reputation and career depend. Fighting means not conceding to the fixed mindset and capitulating to the stock answers, "The organization is not ready" or "I need to lower my revenue or raise my spending." Attitudes are significant inhibitors to OV, and I gave up too soon. As Morpheus in *The Matrix* said, "It's one thing to know the path; it's another to follow it." I didn't follow the path.

The era of long-term survival through increased efficiency is waning. It's morphing into an age where there is no sustainable advantage, only persistent advantage, which is cyclical, ongoing, and demands that leaders act amidst uncertainty. This means going on the offensive. It's not failing fast but learning fast—and then adapting.

 Gold Nugget: It's not failing fast but learning fast—and then adapting.

OV requires speed, but it's about much more than merely moving faster in response to changes in the external environment or spotting disruption more quickly and accurately. OV calls for a new mindset about how to redeploy capital and resources into areas vital to the company's future success—before the impact of the investment is known. This is a mindset of continual learning. Even when you're at the top of your game, you study the tape the morning after the last game you won, and you learn.

If You Don't Know, You Know

The thinking problem permeates company meeting rooms, but it should not permeate all decisions. Be sure to separate reversible from irreversible decisions.

For example, most decisions regarding moving a product or service into testing are reversible. If the test doesn't work out, you're out some time and money, but it doesn't undermine business as usual. Many decisions we make in our personal and professional lives are reversible and should be made quickly. Irreversible decisions, however, are a different story. These decisions may not be completely irreversible but very difficult to unwind, such as code changes in legacy IT systems, acquisitions, or marriage. In these cases, I had a wise manager at UPS who told me, "If you don't know, you know." I've used this decision-making framework with much success and have passed my manager's advice on to my kids. As most decisions are reversible, the mantra allows you to overcome the thinking problem and act with speed and agility more often.

 Truth Bomb: If you don't know, you know.

The same applies to legacy businesses. In chapter 3, I will lay out the complete system for operating a legacy business in an age of disruptive innovations.

What?

Get your mindset right and success will follow.

So What?

The status quo is a mighty force that will pull you to the middle where it's safe. Actions taken to "create the new" will fade like a pebble in a pond when status quo mindsets rule. The OV discovery process requires leaders with a mindset comfortable with uncertainty, able and willing to pivot as information is created, with the fortitude to look past the naysayers.

Now What?

Critically evaluate your mindset and work with other leaders to do the same. Is your mindset aligned to move at the speed of the challenge?[34] Take inventory of your biases. What mental barriers are holding you and your team back from achieving your persistent advantage? The new mindset will filter through culture, processes, metrics, and rewards allowing your company to operate with Organizational Velocity.

---

[34] I am borrowing the phrase, "moving at the speed of the challenge" from a conversation with a U.S. military general in which he described the different kind of challenges while he was at the European Command, such as high-end Russian issue as well as addressing Isis fighters in the streets of Paris returning from the Middle East.

CHAPTER 3

Unlocking Persistent Advantage

No one can possibly know what is about to happen: it is happening, each time, for the first time, for the only time.

—James Baldwin[1]

The year was 2007. Most Americans had not yet heard of Alibaba.

At that time, Alibaba had a pre-IPO value of about $8 billion, a fraction of the nearly $800 billion it has reached recently.[2] In 2007, Alibaba was essentially an industrial matchmaker, matching businesses in the West that needed things with firms in the East that made things.

I was leading the New Product Concepts groups at UPS at the time, and a manager in our Treasury department came to me with a novel idea: could UPS be a matchmaker? Could we bring the East and the West together?

While Alibaba made its connections electronically, UPS lived at the nodes of a worldwide network. UPS could not only match companies electronically, but its service providers could also physically verify that the businesses were what they said they were. UPS could leverage its expertise today to create a new platform business tomorrow.

And thus, Project Pangea was born: we would reconnect the continents. Our team laid out the known facts, what was possible, and the path to get there.

---

[1] J. Baldwin. 1985. *The Price of the Ticket*. Collected Essays, St. Martin's Press.
[2] "United Parcel Service, Inc. (UPS) Valuation Measures & Financial Statistics," https://finance.yahoo.com/quote/UPS/key-statistics/ (accessed September 30, 2020).

The idea was patented, and the excitement built. And then the hammer dropped, "That's not what we do," followed by the coup de grâce, "Can you guarantee a return on investment within a year? Why would I invest our limited capital for an uncertain return when I could invest it in a more certain, albeit limited, return?"

My biggest obstacle was the entrenched mindset of successful senior managers. It was whack-a-mole for any emerging idea that explored possibilities outside of the core business.

"That's not our business" could be the most destructive phrase in the corporate world. These four words encapsulate all the cognitive barriers of dominant logic and marketing myopia discussed earlier. Pangea would move UPS upstream in the buying process, bumping up against the dominant logic of the firm.

 Truth Bomb: "That's not our business" could be the most destructive phrase in the corporate world.

The Alibaba threat was observed but not accepted. This may have been the correct decision. Saying "yes" to everything complicates the execution of anything. However, this acceptance stage is the "danger zone" for many businesses. Few leaders get fired for saying "no" to the right thing. The opposite is not true, and fear is a powerful motivator influencing what environmental signals are accepted. To "create the new," organizational velocity (OV) leaders must fight through that fear and lean into "yes" until the environmental feedback supports a "no."

Creating Persistent Advantage

In the latter part of the 20th century, a popular business objective was creating a "sustainable competitive advantage," meaning a firm could defend its market advantage in the future;[3] build a unique mousetrap; and then, protect it with a high castle and a wide moat. Deep into the later years

---

[3] M.E. Porter and Competitive Advantage. 1985. "Creating and Sustaining Superior Performance," *Competitive Advantage* 167.

of the Third Industrial Revolution, the 1980s and 90s, the concept made perfect sense.

Today's disruptive technologies obviate the very idea of sustainable advantage; it's a construct from a different time and a concept that is all but dead.

The more relevant term is *persistent* advantage. This concept infers that any advantage a firm gains is temporary and that long-term success (in reality, survival) requires the consistent discovery and building of new advantages. Ergo, going on the offensive. OV is the *modus vivendi*, a way of living, for persistent advantage. Today, the only competitive advantage is to learn and react faster than your competitor—constantly. At all times.

> Gold Nugget: Organizational Velocity is the *modus vivendi*, a way of living, for persistent advantage. Today, the only competitive advantage is to learn and react faster than your competitor—constantly. At all times.

Persistent advantage is not about neglecting your knitting, your current model. Persistent advantage is not based on the success of the past or what a firm *thinks* is going to happen. It's about the present moment, what's happening in current reality. The only way to test a novel concept is to do it. To try it. To pilot it. And then learn and react faster than your competitors. This is the essence of persistent advantage—and the engine of OV.

Persistent advantage is built on what is called "optionality." As a noun, the word *optionality* means "the potential for options."[4]

As there is no moat wide or deep enough to stop the inevitable invaders (the accessibility to technology by all companies has made that obvious), companies need to create a portfolio of options. The more options a company has, the better suited it is to deal with unpredictability, if not uncertainty. Leaders can remain calm when others panic because they have choices. Nothing feels more stifling than facing limited and stark choices

---

[4] "Optionality Definition and Meaning," *Collins English Dictionary*. Harper Collins Publishers. www.collinsdictionary.com/us/dictionary/english/optionality

based on dramatic shifts in the market or economy. In the Old Testament, Ecclesiastes 11:2 states, "Invest in seven ventures, yes in eight; you do not know what disaster may come upon the land" (New International Version). Eight ventures mean optionality, which also provides leaders the flexibility to capitalize on change. Keeping options open requires a diversity of knowledge, perspective, analysis, and skills. No executive aspires to sell something no one wants, but more are finding themselves in just that position as change accelerates. The only way to avoid it is to develop a portfolio of options.

 Gold Nugget: Persistent advantage is built on optionality.

During the COVID-19 crisis of 2020, Microsoft founder Bill Gates announced that the Gates Foundation would help fund factories for seven promising coronavirus vaccines.[5] Gates knew that only one or two of the seven factories would be successful. Building factories serially, one at a time as each is needed, is more efficient but not more effective. Efficiency moves at a snail's pace. Optionality dramatically increases the likelihood of more success sooner. The hope was that one vaccine would work, with a factory ready to ramp up production immediately. Bill Gates created options using a process that is now familiar: building a large network to create new opportunities for observing behavior through small-bet pilots. Options ensure a higher likelihood of success.

Bill and Melinda Gates' approach is no different from that of Amazon or Alibaba. Their leaders designed cell-based networks of innovation to create ideas and develop and shepherd them into the piloting phase. Only a few ideas are commercialized, with one or two becoming a part of the core business. If that. On its face, the process seems incredibly wasteful, but it is one of the surest ways to create opportunities for tremendous growth. Amazon, in particular, funds multiple pilots attacking

---

[5] Isobel Asher Hamilton, "Bill Gates is funding 7 new factories for potential coronavirus vaccines," *World Economic Forum* (April 6, 2020). https://www.weforum.org/agenda/2020/04/bill-gates-7-potential-coronavirus-vaccines/

the same opportunity so they don't lose time with a serial approach. The payoff is the speed of learning, which translates into speed to market.

Which, as we all know, has led to the Amazonification of the world.

What Is Your Doctrine?

What was virtually sacrosanct to Amazon was rarely tolerated at UPS, the "tightest ship in the shipping business." Investing in multiple companies or projects to attack the same problem simply wasn't part of the UPS "doctrine." I led the Corporate Venture Capital group at UPS, whose purpose was to invest in startups that grew UPS "knowledge capital" on new technologies or business models. At the time, UPS had already invested in an innovative on-demand delivery company called Deliv. I wanted UPS to invest in another company simultaneously. Roadie, a competitor to Deliv, was trying to solve the same problem but with a different model using crowd-sourced drivers instead of contractors. UPS eventually invested in Roadie, but it took a Herculean effort. In a publicly traded company like UPS, limiting options is much more efficient than pursuing optionality. As it turned out, Deliv shut down operations in 2020, and Roadie was acquired by UPS in 2021.

My point isn't to criticize UPS; great companies have to make tough choices about their investment dollars. However, every family-owned, private equity-owned, or publicly traded company has a doctrine of growth, an implicit or explicit belief system that influences its decisions. As I touched on in chapter 2, a culture of efficiency is often the default doctrine baked into many companies that enjoyed success in the Third Industrial Revolution. Creating organizational velocity requires firms to break out of that efficiency-above-all mindset and embrace the fluid reality of optionality.

Agility and Speed

A leader captaining her ship through the waters of unpredictability cannot thrive with a rigid mindset.

Drug companies rarely, if ever, worked with other drug companies. That is a kind of rigidity. The COVID-19 crisis of 2020 compelled two drug companies, Gilead Sciences and Roche Holding, to partner in a study to pair Roche's immune suppressor Actemra with Gilead's anti-viral drug Remdesivir. Remdesivir was the only drug early on effective in treating coronavirus patients with severe pneumonia.[6] Perilous times create strange bedfellows, or in this case, new bedfellows who amended their doctrines. When companies bust out of the rigidity of entrenched company culture, they often create new business relationships, models, and opportunities. Flexibility may cost more than rigidity in the short term, but the payoff is the ability to pivot during economic transitions and turbulence.

OV is a *fluid* approach to operating a business that enables fast learning. It is the capability to observe, accept (or not), and act (or not) on threats and opportunities facing the firm with speed and agility. A sports equivalent is the 400-meter hurdles, which requires speed and agility to clear obstacles. One obstacle for OV businesses is how to process mountains of data quickly. Because massive data sets can't be processed manually, organizations must have digital systems and scientists in place to sift through that information. A quick LinkedIn search of "data scientist" quickly reveals the companies that are set up to observe and quickly react to threats. Amazon yielded 12000+ "data scientist" results; Macy's yielded a mere 32.[7]

To thrive amidst the disruption of the Fourth Industrial Revolution requires more than speed. You also need the right information to be able to act quickly and with conviction at the right time. Elon Musk personifies acting with a sense of urgency. A popular story tells of a Boring Company meeting where Musk asked his staff how long it would take to remove cars from the lot and begin digging the first tunnel. "Two weeks" was the answer. Musk asked them to get started that day and see how big a hole they could dig between then and Sunday afternoon, running 24

---

[6] www.bloomberg.com/news/articles/2020-05-28/roche-partners-with-gilead-in-covid-trial-of-drug-\\\combination

[7] "Data Scientist Jobs in United States," *LinkedIn.* www.linkedin.com/jobs/search/?geoId=103644278&keywords=macys%2C%20data%20scientist&location=United%20States (accessed June 20, 2021).

hours a day. Reportedly, within three hours the cars were gone and there was a hole in the ground.[8]

OV is not just about being fast. It is a series of forward-moving feedback loops, which influence both the speed and quality of learning as well as the ability to act at the most opportune time. The best mover isn't necessarily the first. The best mover is the organization that is moving when the time is right. This sometimes means learning from the pioneers to build something better. Apple didn't offer the first digital music player, Zoom wasn't the first video call platform, and the first Tesla did not roll off the lot until 12 years after GM offered the first electric car.

I once moderated an e-commerce panel at a conference called ICE (Internet Commerce Exposition) in the late 1990s. One of my panelists was Marc Randolph, the co-founder of a relatively new company called Netflix. This was in the early days when Netflix shipped DVDs (even today, Netflix will still send a DVD to your door!). In the late 1990s, streaming wasn't an option; high Internet speeds that enable it were still only a dream. Even in 2007, when streaming began, bandwidth in population-dense communities was maddeningly slow.

I asked Randolph about the viability of the business model long term. "I don't know what the right business model is going to be," he said.

Randolph didn't know the future, but he and his team were willing to learn and adapt quickly to what was working. That's the key; learning and adapting quickly. OV is learning from what is happening in real-time instead of trying to envision the future and plan backward from there. You can't plan what you don't know. Leaders practicing OV are adept at reading current events and converting that information into better actions.

 Truth Bomb: You can't plan what you don't know.

---

[8] N. Strauss. 2017. "Elon Musk: The Architect of Tomorrow," *Rolling Stone*.

The Tempo Hack

A key component of Boyd's OODA Loop model referenced in chapter 2 is creating a faster tempo or rhythm than your adversary. Compressing one's sense of time while stretching out your adversary's sense of time causes confusion and disorder, forcing the enemy to over- or under-react. In essence, it's moving from defense (passively waiting for what may come) to offense (initiating change and thus creating new opportunities). Consider how Tesla is constantly pushing software updates to their vehicles while achieving exponential improvements in battery cost and performance. Tesla is an MMA fighter. Just when the incumbents think they're catching up to Tesla, it unleashes a foot to the face.

The OODA Loop builds on the Blitzkrieg philosophy of "rapidity," the notion of moving aggressively and then pulling back to create the illusion that you are bigger than you are. This keeps the enemy off guard. In one of the most decisive victories of the Gulf War, Army Lt. Gen. H. R. McMaster decided to push beyond "73 Easting" (past the "limit of advance," where the plan was to stop attacking) and caught the Iraqis by surprise. McMaster's sporadic attacks with a smaller troop in inclement weather and unfamiliar terrain wiped out the Iraqi resistance.[9]

The Blitzkrieg philosophy stipulates each level of the organization has its own OODA Loop. At higher levels (at the theater level, for example), the time cycle may be slower, but at the lower (platoon) levels, the time cycle increases, and the number of events to be considered increases. Feedback loops ensure a large variety of conceptual lenses to capture or understand current reality. In the military version of the OODA Loop, units are organized in semi-autonomous cells, avoiding rigid hierarchical, top-down structures that are neither fast nor nimble. Ultimately, Blitzkrieg disrupts the plans of the opponent and renders them irrelevant. This changes the nature of war by disrupting the preconceived plans of the adversary.

---

[9] T. Gibbons-Neff. February 21, 2017. "The Tank Battle that Came to Define the Early Career of Trump's New National Security Adviser," *Washington Post*, www.washingtonpost.com/news/checkpoint/wp/2017/02/21/the-tank-battle-that-came-to-define-the-early-career-of-trumps-new-national-security-adviser/, www.washingtonpost.com

Speed of action is not the only way to create tempo; learning speed is just as impactful. By feeding more information into the observe-accept-act cycle, more learnings and options to act on are created. That's why running three similar pilots at the same time can generate a faster tempo than running one at a time. Consider this scenario. As vice president of new products, you make the seemingly cost-effective decision to launch a single pilot project to test one of three service alternatives. If you choose the wrong alternative, you'll need to start over. Even if you meet the minimum benchmarks to move forward with a commercial offering, you will still never know how it stacks up against the other options. You move forward but with a potentially suboptimal solution. Do that enough, and you'll innovate your way into irrelevancy. That is the perfect example of the tyranny of small decisions, the subject of an essay by Economist Alfred Kahn. He shows how we often make seemingly small, rational decisions that over time become significantly larger in implication but not necessarily for the better.[10]

And yet, it's not merely about a greater volume of ideas. Innovation is not an idea problem, per se; it is a recognition problem. That is, it is the task of knowing. You need to know which opportunity or threat to act on. To be successful in the paradigm of OV, however, a leader must act before the answer is obvious.

 Gold Nugget: Innovation is not an idea problem, per se; it is a recognition problem.

It is the same with companies and new product ideas. They must have a way of identifying the good from the bad, much like what Amazon does with their doctrine that prioritizes customer obsession over other competing metrics such as volume, revenue, and profit.[11] Without a guiding doctrine, the impulse is to pursue everything and accomplish nothing. The issue is not about whether to kill a project; it's about *why*

---

[10] A.E. Kahn. 1966. *The Tyranny of Small Decisions: Market Failures, Imperfections, and the Limits of Economics*, Vol. 19. Kyklos.

[11] "Leadership Principles," *US About Amazon, Amazon*, www.aboutamazon.com/about-us/leadership-principles

the project is killed: Was it because the team *thinks* the customers won't like it or because several iterations were tested with customers, and they confirmed that they didn't like it? Is it because you don't *think* you'll make any money or because the customers say they want your product but they are not willing to pay for it?

This is why velocity is so critical. The "velocity" in OV is speed with purpose. Offering a superior product at just the right time can only be attained through continuous, iterative learning cycles. Further, speed is not absolute; it's relative. One of the benefits of going on offense is putting your competitors "on their heels." They spend time figuring out your next move while you spend time increasing your value to customers.

Technology Alone Won't Win the Day

Technology can help a firm cast a wide net of observation and process the data through complex algorithms at blazing speed to create actionable information. However, since algorithms are coded by humans, at least initially, they suffer the same biases we all do.

 Truth Bomb: All algorithms are biased.

What data is necessary? How is it prioritized? What do you do with it? If the answers to those questions are based on a worldview that is no longer relevant, your algorithms will also be irrelevant. Baseball players, for example, were evaluated for years on similar criteria. Billy Beane of the Oakland A's revolutionized the game when he defied convention and looked at stats that other teams ignored. He also took biases into account. In his book, *The Undoing Project*, Michael Lewis put it this way:[12]

> The market for baseball players was rife with inefficiencies: why? The Oakland front office had talked about "biases" in the market-place: Foot speed was overrated because it was so easy to see, for instance, and a hitter's ability to draw walks was undervalued in

---

[12] M. Lewis. 2016. *The Undoing Project: A Friendship that Changed the World.* Penguin UK.

part because walks were so forgettable—they seemed to require the hitter mainly to do nothing at all. Fat or misshapen players were more likely to be undervalued; handsome, fit players were more likely to be overvalued.

We all have powerful biases that shape our thoughts and actions. One of the most pervasive is confirmation bias, the tendency to look for data that confirms what we already believe and discount data that runs counter to our beliefs.[13] Ask yourself what news anchor you tend to watch the most. Does he or she offer a perspective of current events that align with yours? Most of us like to think we embrace Abraham Lincoln's "team of rivals" approach, but in reality, we don't. I have never seen an executive team or a board that could be considered a "team of rivals." OV leaders need to recognize their biases as much as possible and actively seek information that disconfirms their beliefs.

This is why the acceptance phase of OV is so critical. It helps us become aware of our biases which will help us better determine what to accept and discard. It's a continual evolution. Knowing what to accept is also a powerful reason to ensure true diversity in the executive ranks. Leaders of different races, creeds, colors, sexes, physical characteristics, and sexual orientations all have different lived experiences. If you bring these perspectives together in an environment of acceptance, you can overcome biases that may have been blinding the executive team of potential opportunities. You will see what was previously unseen.

Never Take Down a Fence Without Knowing Why It Was Built

OV requires a company to know the "why" of whatever it plans to change *before* the change. In the early 1990s, UPS wanted to pass on its technology costs to the customer. We added new features to our customer-facing technology every year, but we were not getting paid for them. These additions were considered part of our core package delivery service. I

[13] C.R. Mynatt, M.E. Doherty, and R.D. Tweney. 1977. "Confirmation Bias in a Simulated Research Environment: An Experimental Study of Scientific Inference," *Quarterly Journal of Experimental Psychology* 29, no. 1.

conducted customer research to find a tipping point where customers would see enough value in our technology solution to pay for it separately. When we discovered no tipping point, the research was viewed as a failure. The answer we received from the market did not support the implicit reason the research was approved, to justify charging for solutions that UPS had always offered for free (with package delivery).

Our research had revealed a perception UPS helped create through the years; customers expected technology to be free, baked into the cost of the service. In fact, the technology *was* originally developed to support the package delivery business. If we wanted our customers to pay, we would need to create a *new* entity to develop and sell our advanced technology solutions to our existing customers, apart from package delivery.

The problem? There was no clear "why" to the decision to pass along the cost to the customer.

In his book, *The Thing*, the British journalist G. K. Chesterton introduced a concept that is now called "Chesterton's Fence": you don't remove a fence until you know why it was put up in the first place. Ergo, unless a leader knows why someone has made a decision, he or she can't safely change the decision or conclude that the original reason for the fence was wrong.

 Gold Nugget: Don't remove a fence until you know why it was put up in the first place.

One leader who consistently finds new solutions to old problems is Elon Musk. Musk employs a technique called first-principles thinking to overcome Chesterton's Fence. It gets to the "why" by revealing the ground reality, not what leaders believe is real. In a 2013 interview, Musk explained how SpaceX had used first-principles thinking to find a new way to build better, lower-cost batteries. Rather than looking for a cheaper battery, they took a close look at the battery they were using. They broke down its basic constituents. Then they worked out the cost to take those core materials and assemble a battery themselves. It was only about 13 percent of the original price.[14]

---

[14] https://youtube.com/watch?v=NV3sBlRgzTI

While time-strapped leaders may be hesitant to engage in first-principles thinking, they need to first ask, "Is it time well spent?" Remember that OV is not about absolute speed; it's about relative speed and being right in time. It's being first to market with the best answer, not any answer. Rio, the maker of the first commercially successful digital audio player can attest to that, as can Tivo, Palm, Friendster, Netscape, and a myriad of other companies. OV is hard. OV requires humility enough to allow new thoughts to penetrate our biases. To be open is to be exponential.

Quality Learning

I have previously mentioned Clayton Christensen's comment that the most important information is that which has not yet been created. OV practitioners need to ask what still-to-be-created information will help drive an action that moves the cycle of iteration forward.

The first step is to gather information from the external environment, such as technology, infrastructure, public health, demographics, or other external force or shift. That will reveal threats to respond to or opportunities to pursue. The company must then cycle through another iteration of questions, asking, "Do we accept this change? Is it important? How soon do we need to act? And with what force?"

A company must then generate its own information through testing. This can be a pilot test or proof of concept or direct feedback from customers on a stimulus that the business is pushing. I recently asked an executive of a Fourth Industrial tech company how her company learns and adapts so quickly. She said, "I'm more concerned with high-quality inputs than I am on focusing on outputs these days. What I found is that higher-quality inputs create higher-quality outputs, kind of like [the reverse] of garbage in, garbage out."

She focuses on inputs from specific kinds of customers who exhibit a particular type of behavior or looking for particular outcomes. All input is important, but not all inputs are created equal. She has discovered that tests with a narrower set of customers increase the quality of her learning.

 Truth Bomb: Higher-quality inputs create higher-quality outputs.

The garbage-in, garbage-out problem illustrates the danger of casting a wide net. To move to action, a company must commit to high-quality learning. A well-defined corporate doctrine allows leaders to block out the white noise and focus only on the signals. This leads to high-quality learning. But high-quality learning must translate into high-quality action—the risk of commercializing a new idea. Leaders who accept failure can only learn from it by moving forward. Momentum is key. It's not iterating in place like Alice does for the Red Queen in *Through the Looking Glass*. "Now, here, you see, it takes all the running you can do," the Red Queen said to Alice, "to keep in the same place."[15] There's no advantage to run fast but not go anywhere. That's merely a treadmill.

Because the future is always uncertain, the only way forward is to commercialize the products that have already shown a modicum of customer acceptance. Too many companies pay a lot of intelligent people to come up with fresh ideas that the company has little interest in commercializing. This is a type of innovation theater, which I discussed in chapter 2. The skillset required to commercialize a product is different from creating the original idea and is a critical component of persistent advantage.

I came across a real-life application of this while researching a blockchain project. Walmart Canada had 80 different transportation vendors, each carrying thousands of loads a day. The presenting issue was contract disputes: did the truck arrive on time? Was everything on the truck that the manifest said was on the truck? The disputes were administratively crushing, so Walmart Canada decided to put the contracts on a blockchain system. When the load was delivered, the trucker got paid, and everything cleared—a virtuous cycle. I asked one of the leaders who had helped "pilot" the project, "How did you do this differently, to have all these people to run these pilots?"

"We won't do a pilot or a proof of concept," he said, "unless the company is committed to commercializing it. Then, if we hit the benchmarks, we launch it."

"Why is that important?" I asked.

---

[15] L. Carroll. 2010. *Through the Looking Glass and What Alice Found There.* Penguin UK.

"Because [of the difference between] the technology group that runs the pilot and those in the business who are actually going to use it." He explained that a pilot is like a hobby to those running it. They are less interested in commercializing the product. A few might: "There will be outliers who push the boulder uphill anyway … Most people [in the pilot group] are logically not like that."[16]

Those responsible for rolling out the new product need to be committed upfront; they need skin in the game. If the pilot is commercialized and successful—they have to own the product. Compensation must be tied to success, which I will cover more explicitly in chapter 8.

The Quest

Mouse McCoy was a stunt man, a motorcycle racer who hit the big time when he directed *Act of Valor* (2012), a movie about an elite team of Navy SEALs on a covert mission to recover a kidnapped CIA agent. Since then, Mouse has moved from director to film producer and, now, to entrepreneur. In 2018, Mouse started Hackrod, a tech company with a mission to enable ordinary folks like you and me to design and build 3D models of hotrods using a form of gamification. Think Tony Stark, Iron Man of the Avengers, who created a 3D hologram world. Hackrod allows for multi-location, multi-person collaboration.

The real genius of Hackrod is its partnership with Siemens, which provides the tech (software) and a manufacturing network to enable "gamers" to build the products. Imagine individuals constructing cars the same way Dell allows customers to choose the components going into their personal computer. Hackrod had the vision and built the marketing platform, and Siemens made it happen with its industrial, digital portfolio. Through its partnership, Hackrod is automating and connecting heavy engineering CAD to a manufacturing-ready virtual environment. Siemens built its technology business around empowering large manufacturing companies. Through its collaboration with Hackrod, Siemens is now creating a digital factory that an individual can operate.

---

[16] L. Owen. March 20, 2020. "Chair and CEO of DLT Labs." Interview by Alan Amling.

The partnership with Hackrod does not distract Siemens from its existing business. Hackrod is only one investment in Siemens' more extensive portfolio. The conglomerate is simply paying attention to a new business for advantage—its *next* advantage.

At the end of chapter 2, I argued that OV is both a mindset and an approach, a different way of "doing" business. The new mindset is going on offense rather than simply playing defense, and the right approach is not merely failing fast but learning fast. Faster than your competitors. Siemens is learning fast—launching a new, smaller business accessible to individuals—while not taking the eye off the ball of its existing corporate-centric business. You can too.

What?

Today's disruptive technologies obviate the very idea of sustainable advantage; it's a construct from a different time, and theory is all but dead. The more relevant term is *persistent* advantage. This concept infers that any advantage a firm gains is temporary. Long-term success requires the consistent discovery and building of new advantages.

So What?

Most established organizations play defense, protecting their "moat" while incrementally improving. Persistent advantage requires the firm to go on offense, actively engaging with the external environment to discover new opportunities and create options to pivot to as appropriate.

Now What?

OV is your optionality playbook. Instead of focusing all your effort on protecting the corporate moat, continuously create new moats. You'll put your competitors on roller skates while you make a self-renewing Forever Company.

CHAPTER 4

From Manager to Maestro

If the highest aim of a captain were to preserve his ship, he would keep it in port forever.

—Thomas Aquinas

On December 9, 2020, SpaceX's prototype Starship rocket exploded on impact as it attempted to land. The $200 million unmanned rocket was gone in a flash. Instead of lamenting the explosion or making excuses, SpaceX CEO Elon Musk gushed with enthusiasm over the test results. In a Tweet, he spoke of the "Successful ascent, switchover to header tanks and precise flap control to landing point!" After bulleting what they had learned from the catastrophic landing, Musk Tweeted, "Congrats, SpaceX team, hell yeah!"[1] That is the mindset of an organizational velocity (OV) leader! For Musk, the Starship crash was not a failure. What they learned would instruct their next attempt. More importantly, he made sure the team put their heart and souls into this prototype and came away with a sense of accomplishment that would motivate them to keep trying until they got it right. It was a small thing, but it made all the difference to the team. Laying into the team on Twitter would have thrown sand in the gears of OV. Instead, Musk bathed the gears in oil.

Major General John Shaw, the first head of the U.S. Space Force, faces the daunting challenge of designing a new organization for a new service. The principles of OV are embedded in the cornerstones of his plan: "increased flexibility, being able to move at speed ..." The Space Force is driving decision making to the lowest practical level to empower

---

[1] M. Sheetz. December 09, 2020. "SpaceX's prototype Starship rocket reaches highest altitude yet but lands explosively on return attempt," *CNBC.* www.cnbc.com/2020/12/09/spacex-starship-rocket-sn8-explodes-after-high-altitude-test-flight-.html

managers to make intelligent, risk-prudent decisions but take sufficient risks so they can move forward.[2] Time will tell if Shaw can slice through the bureaucracy, but the mindset of leadership is in the right place.

Victory has a hundred fathers and defeat is an orphan.[3]

This common saying is often true of leaders in large, incumbent organizations. Executives tend to hem and haw when it comes to piloting new ideas. Still, when success arrives, the resumes of those in and around the innovation all include some version of "Created the product concept and led the innovation team resulting in $500MM of new revenue."

There are no bystanders, however, in an incumbent organization that manages to create disruptive innovation. The leader who brings about the change has a steely sense of conviction. A good example comes from the leaders responsible for launching Hulu, the premium streaming service. The innovation was an unlikely alliance between Fox News Corp and NBC.

Peter Chernin drove the disruptive innovation from the News Corp side, while David Zasloff did the same at NBC. Neither was the CEO at their respective entities. Rupert Murdoch was still the CEO of News Corp., and Jeff Zucker was the CEO of NBC. But both Chernin and Zasloff ran the innovation gauntlet with a fierce conviction. Zasloff, especially, had a large personality who, according to those present, would literally pound his chest and say, "This [the Hulu initiative] is a billion-dollar idea. It's going to happen."[4] Jeff Zucker was fully supportive of David Zasloff, and Rupert Murdoch fully supported Peter Chernin, the COO of News Corp.

Executives like Chernin and Zasloff often wait out their entire careers for an idea like Hulu. Then, when they find themselves in a situation where disruption presents an opportunity, they recognize it's

---

[2] www.nationaldefensemagazine.org/articles/2020/8/7/space-force-new-services-future-coming-into-focus

[3] The saying is originally attributed to the Italian diplomat and son-in-law of Mussolini, Count Caleazzo Ciano, circa 1942.

[4] Interview with Jack Kennedy, December 15, 2018.

their big chance. And they become an immovable force. That is, they refuse to back down from driving the change. They place themselves at the center of the chaos churned out by change and take the calculated risks to keep moving forward. Jack Kennedy, who served as Executive Vice President of Strategy and Corporate Development at Fox Interactive Media at the time, described the leaders as being "singularly capable of permitting the big chaos required while not being overrun by internal obstacles."

> Gold Nugget: OV leaders must be singularly capable of permitting the big chaos required while not being overrun by internal obstacles.

I used to think that change came from the top management team, and I was 100 percent wrong. It comes from what can only be described as an immovable force whose conviction overcomes the inertia and resistance endemic in large entities.

Innovation rarely, if ever, is led by the CFO, the CMO, or even the CTO; it's typically the CEO.

Chernin and Zasloff were CEOs of their respective divisions and believed that Hulu could not be a joint venture between News Corp. and NBC; it had to be a separate company. The parties agreed to take capital from a third-party investor with expertise supporting growth companies. Doing so would ensure the company was run with a fiduciary responsibility to itself and not to its partners. In some respects, the decision to separate Hulu as a standalone business inoculated the innovation from the drama of senior management of News Corp. and NBC. It otherwise might have been a train wreck.

Chernin and Zasloff exemplified the traits that create OV. Their brand of leadership can move at a faster tempo amidst the chaos. Their conviction compels them to develop fast-forward buttons for their organizations. These leaders set up their teams to sort through the data at a faster clip (with greater access to data); to move forward at a faster tempo (with higher spending authority); to take educated risks (with compensation tied to new revenue streams); and to continue to learn as they encounter resistance and roadblocks.

Narratives that Matter

While the "fail fast" cliché may make for a snappy slogan at the corporate retreat, the tempo itself creates the risk of chaos, which often causes leaders to trumpet one thing but act differently. For example, at UPS, we had a slogan (for a while) called "moving forward fast," a phrase emblazoned on marketing and investor materials. Once, in front of the CEO in a meeting, I said, "I love the slogan 'moving forward fast.' It's exactly what we need to take the next steps on this project. It will help us move forward fast."

"Whoa, whoa, whoa," he said. "Yes, forward fast, but not too fast!"

The CEO had just signaled to everyone in the room that the slogan was just that: a slogan. It wasn't meant to be acted on and lived out. The CEO's reluctance comes from a common belief among leaders—that too much movement too fast creates chaos. And, in reality, living out the "forward-fast" slogan will create a modicum of chaos. However, the most distinctive characteristic of an OV leader is the ability to inspire and align the team through words *and* actions—even if it kicks up a bit of chaos. This characteristic is captured in John Boyd's term borrowed from the German Army, *schwerpunkt*, which refers to the main focus. For OV to take hold, the CEO must articulate a main focus that is more than simply values, goals, and objectives. *Schwerpunkt* is a doctrine about how the firm will engage its markets and monitor its threats. *Schwerpunkt* lays out the goal and provides the boundaries within which everyone in the firm is free to act. The doctrine sets guidelines for decision making—one that gives permission to act within boundaries toward the same goal.

Consider UPS' latest doctrine under CEO Carol Tomé, "better not bigger." In her first seven months, Tomé raised rates, limited capacity for larger shippers who exceeded their volume forecast, cut capital expenditures by about $2 billion, sold the lower-margin less-than-truckload (LTL) business, and offered voluntary separation packages to over 11,000 non-operations employees. "Better, not bigger" became UPS's *schwerpunkt* not when it was a talking point, but when it was acted on. While I argue that UPS does not yet espouse the doctrine of a Forever Company, there is no doubt that the "new sheriff in town" has aligned the front lines around the new vision. A salesperson no longer has to wonder whether to sign a deal that offers lower profit margins but large volumes. The doctrine is clear: volume at all costs is no longer acceptable. Clear doctrines save sales time in identifying target accounts and negotiating deals. Vague doctrines (e.g., "growth is our top priority" or "focus on fundamentals") cloud decision making and slow down OV.

A key success factor for organizations is the people on the field of battle (closest to the customer) knowing what to do; the doctrine helps them make the best decision for the organization based on the current context and their personal judgment. Think of a flock of starlings. They exhibit a rare combination of speed and scale. The birds coordinate themselves with remarkable agility to find food and avoid attacks—with no apparent leader. Instead, each bird ostensibly follows three basic rules: (1) move to the center, (2) follow your neighbor, and (3) don't collide. "The rules enable each bird to act independently while ensuring the group acts cohesively."[5]

The Amazon Flywheel is a perfect example of the virtuous circle created from a clear doctrine. At Amazon, customer experience reigns supreme. The Amazon Flywheel creates a virtuous circle beginning with customer experience. A better customer experience creates more customer traffic, attracts more sellers with more products, and improves customer experience. Greater volume creates opportunities for economies of scale, which drives down prices and further enhances the customer experience.[6] One Amazon executive put it this way, "What I find is when you start working backward from the customer, you start making decisions really differently. If you are weighing two investments, should I invest in reverse logistics or invest in brokerage. You would ask, 'Which one is driving customer experience versus driving cost out?' You would pick the higher customer experience option, and that would answer the question." A clear *schwerpunkt* reduces the ambiguity that creates friction that slows down OV in a firm.

---

[5] M. Bonchek. 2016. "How Leaders Can Let Go Without Losing Control," *Harvard Business Review* 2.
[6] J.P. Bezos, Amazon 2014 Letter to Shareholders.

Guardrails of Conviction

Leaders can live out their OV slogans only when the slogan becomes an actionable doctrine for those at the front lines of an organization. Ben Baldanza is an OV leader. I crossed paths with Baldanza, the former CEO of Spirit Airlines when UPS hired him to help translate yield management strategies designed for the airline industry to the package delivery industry. While that effort was unsuccessful, his career was just the opposite. Baldanza transitioned through several airline leadership roles to eventually take the helm at struggling Spirit Airlines. He joined Spirit Airlines the year after the fledgling carrier lost $80 million.[7] Spirit's *schwerpunkt* needed a dramatic overhaul, and Baldanza brought it when he was promoted to CEO in 2006. Five years later, Spirit earned 40 percent more per airplane than any other U.S. Airline.

The public saw a trade-off between super low fares and packed flights (with one less lavatory to allow for more seats), high baggage fees, and extra charges for everything from boarding passes to peanuts. Business passengers fled, but leisure travelers flocked to the airline. Spirit now had an identity. It knew what it was, and just as importantly, what it wasn't. Baldanza used to joke that he would someday walk into a Chick-fil-A and scream, "What do you mean you don't sell hamburgers here!"

What the public did not see, however, is what made Baldanza an OV leader. Baldanza said, "People would ask why our model was not replicable, why someone couldn't out-Spirit Spirit. I said they could have the planes, and they can charge for bags and things like that. But I don't believe most airline people have the conviction we have. I felt conviction was our biggest corporate culture asset, conviction that we were doing the right thing. We used to say that we had very clear mirrors in our building, meaning we knew exactly who we were and who we weren't."

 Gold Nugget: Conviction is a corporate asset.

---

[7] R. Walker. January 22, 2020. "If Everyone Hates Spirit Airlines, How Is It Making So Much Money?" *Medium.* https://marker.medium.com/if-everyone-hates-spirit-airlines-how-is-it-making-so-much-money-8c7d13472352

That conviction started with the CEO, but it didn't spread on its own. When Baldanza became CEO, there were 23 officers at Spirit. A year later, there were 12, and none of the original 23 were part of the 12. "You're either on the train," said Baldanza, "or you need to get off the train." So he lured top talent with the opportunity for significant equity growth and gave them the authority to make the necessary changes to become the ultra-low-cost leader.

Spirit's conviction to economic efficiency permeated every corner of the organization. Baldanza had executives cover the cost of their business cards through sponsorships by local businesses featured on the flip side of each person's business card. He took this low-cost approach so seriously he even developed corporate partnerships to cover the costs of special building projects. Spirit boasted an Airbus room, a Pratt and Whitney room, and a Lufthansa boardroom. This conviction had a stunning impact. As vendors tried to squeeze him in negotiations, he would refer to his business card: "If I won't pay for my business cards, what makes you think I'll pay for your increase?" Baldanza says, "Understanding who we were, what we were about and having a strong conviction around that—it's what changed that whole company."[8]

The development of Hulu discussed earlier is another example of conviction. Current CEO of Platform Science and former Fox Interactive Media executive Jack Kennedy recalls the conviction of News Corp. COO Peter Chernin in the early days of Hulu. The naysayers were everywhere, calling the startup "Clown Co."[9] However, his conviction kept the idea of Hulu alive while new partners came on board, and previously intractable problems, such as how to split profits between the platform owners and the content providers, were solved.

There is one crucial caveat to conviction. Ignoring changes in the external environment to keep up a façade is not conviction; it's ignorance or foolish pride. While Spirit's Ben Baldanza saw conviction as a corporate asset, some ancillary products they tried didn't work, so he reversed them. Alternatively, some ancillary products proved more effective than

---

[8] B. Baldanza. May 18, 2020. "CEO, Diemacher LLC, Former CEO, Spirit Airlines." Interview by Alan Amling.
[9] Ibid.

they thought, which changed their plans on ticket price reductions.[10] Sense and respond; it's the OV way.

The Missing Jewel: Risk

Many executives survive the climb up the corporate ladder because of their expertise in risk mitigation. They've seen others get knocked off the fast track by one public misstep. While at UPS, I took on many speaking gigs outside the company; I loved doing them. Most executives avoided such engagements. Their reasoning was the risk/reward. They saw only the risk of saying something that landed them in trouble and undervalued the greater good to tell the company's story.

Prospect theory describes the way people choose between alternatives that entail risk, when the probability of outcomes is known.[11] The theory explains why people buy insurance, pay a premium above the expected loss, and participate in lotteries, with a negative expected value but tremendous payoff. The value function (for example, speaking on behalf of the company) is steeper for losses than the gains, indicating that losses outweigh gains in executives' minds. Their desire to avoid loss exceeded their desire to secure gain.

Executives become executives in part because of their aversion to risk. This aversion only increases with time as they near the apotheosis of their careers. What CEO wants to end their career taking on a risk that fails?

I interviewed Chuck Adair, a former Vice Chairman for BMO Capital markets who sits on several publicly traded companies' boards, calling this phenomenon "runway bias."[12] Executives, late in their careers, tend to paint too rosy a picture of the future. Runway bias refers to the short runway that senior executives have that distorts their thinking about the future. Executives in their early sixties, with only a few years to retirement, avoid envisioning a scenario in which their tenure ends

---

[10] B. Baldanza. June 22, 2021. "CEO, Diemacher LLC, Former CEO, Spirit Airlines." Interview by Alan Amling.

[11] D. Kahneman and A. Tversky. 2013. "Prospect Theory: An Analysis of Decision Under Risk," In *Handbook of the Fundamentals of Financial Decision Making: Part I*. World Scientific.

[12] Adair, Interview.

badly. Their power, their prestige, their ego, the esprit de corps among the senior team—it all keeps them from facing reality. Their bias prevents them from looking out far enough and clearly looking at the facts. They "feel" their short runway and back away from taking risks.

Essentially, most executives are no different; they are more afraid of loss than motivated by gain. An ambiguity-averse individual would instead choose an alternative where the probability distribution of the outcomes is known over one where the probabilities are unknown.

This leads us to the larger question. What's the actual governing narrative of the organization? Companies trumpet their mission statement, but often it's the less-explicit subtext of efficiency (and consequently profit margins) that drives the story. When UPS was still the American Messenger Company, its founder, Jim Casey, challenged his employees: "Are we working for money alone? If so, there is no surer way not to get it."[13] Any organization whose default narrative is efficiency only (maximizing shareholder value only) will struggle to create a culture of OV.

Larry Fink at Blackrock believes that companies must serve a larger social purpose and that long-term shareholder value is accomplished by having a sense of purpose. BlackRock went public in 1999 at $14/share and eclipsed $600/share in August 2020 at the height of the COVID-19 pandemic.

Amazon famously told investors that they would prioritize long-term customer growth over near-term profits right from the start. In his 1997 Letter to Shareholders, Jeff Bezos wrote:

> We first measure ourselves in terms of the metrics most indicative of our market leadership: customer and revenue growth, the degree to which our customers continue to purchase from us on a repeat basis, and the strength of our brand. We have invested and will continue to invest aggressively to expand and leverage our customer base, brand, and infrastructure as we move to establish an enduring franchise. Because of our emphasis on the long term, we may make decisions and weigh tradeoffs differently than some companies.[14]

---

[13] J. Casey. 1985. *Our Partnership Legacy*. United Parcel Service.

[14] Amazon. 1998. *1997 Letter to Shareholders*. https://ir.aboutamazon.com/annual-reports-proxies-and-shareholder-letters/default.aspx

Amazon would never focus on profits or shareholder returns directly, Bezos explained. Instead, it would focus 100 percent of its energy on building value for its customers. Much of Wall Street, of course, was skeptical of the still-unprofitable company that had just gone public. Amazon didn't pay dividends and didn't seem to care about becoming profitable. This singular act of conviction that it would not focus on profits gave Amazon a "pass" on Wall Street that no other public companies enjoy.

More amazing even than Amazon's ascendancy is the question, "Why hadn't anyone thought like this before?"

Between 1995 and 2018, in Amazon's Letters to Shareholders, the word "customer" (or "customers") appears 443 times, which makes it the most common word in all 23 letters by far (omitting words like "and" or "the," for example). By way of comparison, the word "Amazon" appears 340 times. Comparatively, "shareholder" and "shareholders" get a total of 53 mentions. Add investor and investors, and it's another eight. "Competition" and its derivatives appear just 28 times across 23 letters. And quite a few of them aren't really referring to competitors; they're some variation of "Amazon's competitive advantage is …"[15]

Clearly, the center of gravity of Amazon is the customer. Not efficiency. Not profits.

Freedom with Limits

Even today, most large organizations are run top-down. They are the antithesis of responsive and agile, two characteristics of younger, Fourth Industrial Revolution companies that eat away at the edges of today's incumbent companies. No one is advocating for the WeWork style of laissez-faire management with a work culture more akin to a rock concert—indeed, I'm not.[16] But OV at its best is coordinated action—

---

[15] B. Murphy. April 13, 2019. "I Ran the Full Text of Jeff Bezos's 23 Amazon Shareholder Letters Through a Word Cloud Generator, and the Insights Were Astonishing | Inc.com." *Inc.*www.inc.com/bill-murphy-jr/i-ran-full-text-of-jeff-bezoss-23-amazon-shareholder-letters-through-a-word-cloud-generator-insights-were-astonishing.html

[16] www.newyorker.com/culture/culture-desk/the-rise-and-fall-of-wework

with significant autonomy and responsibility pushed to the edges of the organization. Only the CEO can create this kind of environment—establishing the expectation that all of us are better than any of us.

 Truth Bomb: All of us are better than any of us.

Of course, this requires a degree of trust. The trick is understanding what needs to be controlled and what does not. Finances cannot be controlled at the edges because employees only have a limited view of the organization. They see the tail and not the elephant. Much of decision making, however, is best done at the edges. Today's corporations need more balance. Efficiency is important but not sufficient. Companies need to be constantly evolving, which means they are in an exploration phase 24 × 7 × 365. This requires talented individuals to be able to act with freedom but within boundaries. With financial controls, the challenge is where to draw the line on spending authority. The less the authority to spend, the more suffocating the environment will be. The greater it is, the more the company is exposed to rogue employees. Deciding where to draw that line is one of the most critical decisions that the senior management team will make. Wherever the line is drawn, it must be at a place that gives those at the edges freedom to explore and take some calculated risks.

In this chapter, I argue that only the CEO can create a responsive culture that fosters OV. In that sense, only the CEO can create and shape the doctrine that pushes decision making to the edges of the organization. I interviewed an Army general who changed how he saw his role as he advanced in his career:

My role evolved from being like the chess master to the role of gardener ... the chess master is reaching onto the chessboard and reaching all the way down and moving every piece, right? Deeply involved in the movement of every piece on the chessboard. Today that'll never work. ... the real role of a leader now is to create a garden if you will, in which many leaders can flourish. And you've got to water that garden, fertilize that garden. And what that means is you've got to give them resources. You've got to give them focus, guidance, direction, but at the end of the day, they're going to run the organization or whatever piece of the organization they own. And that's a big shift in terms of the role of a leader.[17]

When a leader moves from being a taskmaster to a gardener, he creates an environment of freedom, and the organization becomes more flexible. This is the essence of OV. Of course, there is always the danger that a well-functioning corporation can be set on the wrong target. Organizations must pivot as they learn.

The Boomerang Effect

OV leaders bring out the best in their people and give credit to people whenever appropriate. A universal phenomenon that I've witnessed in my career and personal life is what I call "The Boomerang Effect." You can't give away credit, support, and love—if it's done sincerely, it will come back to you. In a 1959 plant managers conference, UPS CEO Jim Casey said, "Once the people you deal with come to recognize that what you do springs from an honest heart, they will be surprisingly strong in their support for you. They will believe what you say. They will do what you want. They will give you their loyalty. They will trust and follow you."[18] That is the essence of an OV leader.

 Truth Bomb: You can't give away credit, support, and love—if it's done sincerely, it will come back to you.

Executive training too often cripples effective leaders, so they can't pivot. Leaders internalize the axiom, "If you give up too soon, you'll look weak," even if they know that their choice or direction is wrong. Giving up will make it look like their judgment is off. So, instead of pivoting, they march down an inevitable path of doom. Perception drives so much of

---

[17] B. Garrett. February 20, 2019. "Strategic Advisor, GGS LLC, Former Lieutenant General—Deputy Commander, US Army." Interview by Alan Amling.
[18] Ibid.

corporate decision making. I once interviewed David Kidder, co-founder and CEO of Bionic, who captured the essence of the problem: "Your executives are lying to you. And it's your fault as a CEO. Because you've given them no choice."[19]

Let's say, for example, an executive requests $500,000 for a project with a certain intended outcome. Six months later, she says, "Based on what we learned, we shouldn't be heading this direction. We should be heading North, not Northeast. We need another 30 percent in funding."

This is the response she would probably get:

Why didn't you know that? I heard from so and so that this was heading south three weeks ago.

If she responds, "We didn't know that at the time," she is dead in the water. And so is the project. If her project needs to be revectored and funded accordingly, her tacit goal will not be to create constructive dialogue and debate. Instead, she will spin the presentation as best as she can and get the hell out of there, hopefully unscathed. Everyone in the room will follow the CEO's lead.

An OV CEO might respond with these words: "So you were expecting to find this, and you found that. Why did you find that? Okay. So, based on that finding, what do you know now that you didn't know before? And how is that going to impact what you do next? Okay. Well, tell me what you recommend then. Okay. Well, that makes sense."

And then the CEO adds, "This is a learning journey."

The leader must clarify that this is not learning for learning's sake but in pursuit of a focused outcome. The CEO sets the tone. If she doesn't, the sharks around the table will smell blood; the project will collapse and leave the manager scarred. All the forward-fast and failing-fast rhetoric is out the door. As long as the project fails due to information that was not known prior or should have been known, OV allows for and even expects the target may not be hit on the first try. Or potentially, the second and

---

[19] Kidder, Interview.

third. Leaders should not fire anyone for missing the mark, as long as each attempt gains new information that gets closer to it.

So what should be considered a failure? If the manager in the above example wasn't able to answer the leader's probing questions, that's a failure. The manager is looking at a transfer or demotion. An egregious (ethical) failure would warrant termination.

On the other hand, if she were able to say, "This is what I've learned. This is how I have to pivot to stay on course towards the goal," an OV leader would applaud her.

 Gold Nugget: The only failure is not learning from actions taken.

As I have argued in previous chapters, the data for hitting the target doesn't exist yet in these projects. If the data did exist, the organization wouldn't be funding the pilot or proof of concept. The nature of "pilot" and "proof of concept" is that the data hasn't yet been created! There's no failure if the first proof of concept doesn't pan out. That's normal. That's expected. Perhaps the only other way to fail in a pilot is to set up the test in a way that doesn't enable the team to learn.

Learning and pivoting demands that a leader becomes a gardener: nurturing an environment of freedom to make decisions and to have access to data.

The Humility Requirement

Flexibility and the ability to learn after a miss is often a corollary of humility. For an executive, humility is, in part, an openness to listening to what he or she doesn't want to hear. Listening begins with curiosity: "Tell us about what you learned?"

In chapter 3, I told the story about researching a new technology offering while at UPS. The original idea was to create new revenue streams from technology that UPS was already providing its customers. My conclusion was that, based on the findings, "as long as the offerings come from UPS, our customers believe they should be part of the value proposition." I proposed a spinoff company, but the response was, "That's not our business. We're a shipping company, not a software company."

The leadership's decision made complete sense in the pre-Fourth Industrial Revolution, pre-Cloud world, in which defending the castle (shipping) was the highest priority. Looking back, UPS missed an opportunity to create logistics software, one of its core competencies. Many leaders struggle to pivot, afraid to risk. There's an escalation of commitment. When a manager presents, "We set out to find this, but we discovered that it is not going to work that way. We have to pivot this other way and get more funding to test whether the pivot could even work." Sooner or later, the CFO or COO is going to say, "We believed you last time. Why should we believe you this time?"

The crux of disruption is the difference between what should happen and what does happen.

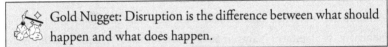 Gold Nugget: Disruption is the difference between what should happen and what does happen.

It takes gritty leaders willing to risk their reputation, not knowing what the outcome will be. Leading disruption requires a humility that emanates out of something more than status or power. Both of these are fleeting. OV leaders hire similarly willing people to risk and be humble—elements of a renaissance leader. I interviewed Mark Kvamme, a venture capitalist, who hired people based on their humility and ability to take on risks. When vetting a person for a partnership with his VC, he would ask, "What is the biggest risk that you've taken?" One interviewee responded with something like, "I had offers to Harvard and MIT, and I decided to go to MIT."[20] It was clear the person had no concept of risk.

Another applicant answered the same question this way: "I was accepted to MIT, and I was accepted to this tiny little college in Indiana specializing in insurance actuary. I wanted to be an insurance actuary, so I said no to MIT, despite its unparalleled reputation." Arguably, it was a riskier move going to a no-name school. But it showed Kvamme his proclivity toward risk: "If you're not willing to take personal risks, you won't take corporate risks." A hallmark of an OV leader is making bold moves—scary moves—that don't necessarily guarantee profitable outcomes.

[20] M. Kvamme. December 09, 2020. "Co-Founder and Partner at Drive Capital." Interview by Alan Amling.

Truth Bomb: If you're unwilling to take personal risks, you won't take corporate risks.

Founder's Mentality

Most executives will not follow in President Lincoln's footsteps and create a team of rivals, appointing opponents to senior teams. We tend to surround ourselves with people who think like us, agree with us, and have had similar experiences. Often, unfortunately, the fiefdom also includes people who look like us. Data and people who take opposing views are easily marginalized.

In my research, the leaders who recognized and broke out of the fiefdoms that they had created had what can only be called a "founder's mentality."[21] Shantanu Narayen at Adobe and Satya Nadella at Microsoft are two examples of CEOs who were not founders but had a founder mentality. Shantanu boldly moved Adobe from selling software licenses to selling subscriptions, a controversial decision at the time. Satya was a long-time Microsoft employee who changed Microsoft from the inside out. Every organization has people with a "founder's mentality," pushing the envelope, going the extra mile. If leaders don't embrace a founder's mentality, then when their truth is ridiculed or violently opposed, they fold, or worse yet, never bring their truth to light. That's why you see most innovation coming from founder-led companies whose leaders also have a founder's mentality. They're owners in the noblest sense. They created the company. They're secure and thus bold.

A 2016 study of Fortune 500 companies showed that those companies tended to be more innovative when the founder still plays a significant role (CEO, chairman, board member, owner, and advisor). As a result, they generated 31 percent more patents, created more valuable patents, and were more likely to make bold investments to renew or

---

[21] C. Zook and J. Allen. 2016. *The Founder's Mentality: How to Overcome the Predictable Crises of Growth*. Harvard Business Review Press.

adapt their business model.[22] I interviewed one of the executives for Cox Communications, about a recent innovation: "Did you have to go through some committees? What was the process to move this forward?"

"We made a short pitch to the senior management," he said, "and they come back with, 'Yeah, let's do it. It's the right thing to do,' and they moved forward."

That move-quick-with-conviction is the essence of the founder's mentality, and it creates OV.

The Disruptor Trifecta

I came up with the phrase "disruptor trifecta" shown in Figure 4.1 to capture the idea that a leader of an incumbent organization must possess three requirements for leading innovation. He or she must be smart, knowledgeable, and technology fluent. Great leaders have always been smart (e.g., possess good judgment) and knowledgeable (know their business). There's a third requirement for success in today's digital world: technology fluency.

The first two are a slam dunk for most senior leaders at incumbent firms. Too often, though, "tech fluency" is missing and designated to a "tech team." However, leaders are blinded to digitally enabled alternatives

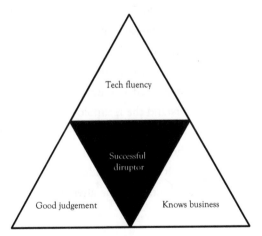

Figure 4.1 Disruptor trifecta

---

[22] J.M. Lee, J. Kim, and J. Bae. 2016. "Founder CEOs and Innovation: Evidence from S&P 500 Firms," Available at SSRN 2733456

without tech fluency, leading to a death march of sub-optimal decisions. More bluntly, many executives who should be leading their firms through the transition to the Fourth Industrial Revolution do not have the tech fluency to see what's possible. Moreover, a 2021 research study analyzing over 1,300 large enterprises with "digitally savvy" executive teams found they "outperformed comparable companies without such teams by more than 48 percent based on revenue growth and valuation."[23]

The concept of tech fluency is not about senior executives knowing how to code machine learning algorithms. However, emerging technology must be understood at more than a superficial level. A good test might be whether an executive can teach a group of non-technology professionals what these new technologies are, why they are essential, and how they change what is possible.

> Gold Nugget: Effective leaders demonstrate all three character-istics of the Disruptor Trifecta—good judgment, know their business, and tech-savvy.

A veteran technology executive explained the challenge facing leaders with little technology fluency: "Because of the evolution of technology … the people in charge of these businesses are facing risks that they don't have a visceral and deep understanding of [the technology]. And they're still in charge of all these businesses." The challenge is to connect the business model and the technology with absolute precision. For too long, IT has traditionally been categorized as a function. Many executives don't feel as if they need to understand the technology: "I don't need to know how the clock works. I just want to know what time it is." The problem is if a leader doesn't know how the clock works, they may think that the time is EST when, in fact, it's GMT. Leaders need to understand the context of technology, the inputs, and the alternatives and to be able to challenge assumptions.

---

[23] P. Weill, S.L. Woerner, and A.M. Shah. 2021. "Does Your C-Suite Have Enough Digital Smarts?," *MIT Sloan Management Review* 62, no. 3.

And, yet, what aging executive has 10,000 hours to master such technology fluency?[24] So many of today's leaders of innovative companies started in the tech industry or are digital natives (born after 1981). The issue, of course, isn't that non-natives can't learn what they need to know. Too often, the real issue is pride. Leadership doesn't want to look foolish, ask questions, or look less than "all-knowing." The OV leader must live at the nexus of efficiency and exploration, experience and openness, pragmatism and idealism. This is uncomfortable and belies the education and experience that propelled most executives to their current leadership roles. No MBA program can prepare any person adequately for leading amidst the Fourth Industrial Revolution. The nexus is uncomfortable because of uncertainty. Moving from what you know to the vulnerability of what you don't is essential to leading a company to a more innovative future.

What?

OV is a way of life that must be driven top-down.

So What?

Command and control leaders won't sustain an OV organization where managers have autonomy within boundaries. Humble leaders demonstrating a founder's mentality allow employees to blossom.

Now What?

Identify the people in your organization that demonstrate OV leadership qualities and put them in positions to put those qualities into action. Then, work the OV Leader Criteria (Good Judgement, Knows Business, Tech Fluent, Bold Vision, Acts with Conviction, Founders Mentality, Humble) into your hiring and promotion plans.

---

[24] Malcolm Gladwell's 10,000 hour concept has been challenged, but it's still a good metaphor for learning. http://graphics8.nytimes.com/images/blogs/freakonomics/pdf/DeliberatePractice%28PsychologicalReview%29.pdf

CHAPTER 5

It's Board, Not Bored

Not everything that counts can be counted, and not everything that can be counted counts.

—Albert Einstein

It was the wonderful American blues singer Albert King who first recorded the classic, "Born Under a Bad Sign" in 1967. The best line of the song is, "If it wasn't for bad luck, I wouldn't have no luck at all." Starting in 2018, Boeing, the great aerospace company, had a string of what might be called "no luck at all." The Boeing 737 MAX entered service in 2017, and in October 2018, a 737 MAX carrying 189 passengers crashed after take-off. Five months later, another 737 MAX crashed after taking off with 157 passengers.

It wasn't luck at all, bad or otherwise, however. With two plane crashes in five months and 346 passengers dead, Boeing scrambled to find answers. The reports from both crashes faulted plane design as one of the factors.[1] In the 737 MAX, apparently, there had been some flight control changes, which many 737 pilots said they had not learned about until after the second crash in March 2019.[2] Some said Boeing omitted the changes in some of the flight manuals and should have required special training for the pilots. While Boeing initially said that there was no

---

[1] "Boeing 737 Max Lion Air Crash Caused by Series of Failures," *BBC News.* www.bbc.com. www.bbc.com/news/business-50177788 (accessed October 25, 2019).

[2] P. Robinson and J. Johnsson. n.d. "Two 737 Max Crashes in Five Months Put Boeing's Reputation on the Line—Bloomberg," *Bloomberg BusinessWeek.* www.bloomberg.com/news/features/2019-03-13/two-737-max-crashes-in-five-months-put-boeing-s-reputation-on-the-line

additional training needed for the 737 MAX, the company reversed its position over time.[3]

During this tumultuous period for the Fortune 500 company, there is no record in the minutes of the Boeing Board of Directors that the problem was discussed or that any board member of this prestigious company asked any questions of the CEO. At least in the official board meeting minutes, there was never a recorded discussion of the issues with the 737 MAX.[4] As a result of the two crashes, some pundits argued that many pilots were losing some of their basic flying skills with all the automation.[5] Wouldn't you think that as a board member of an airline manufacturer with two crashes in five months, you would ask the CEO about that? Wouldn't you talk to your two biggest customers, Southwest and American, and ask them for feedback from the pilots on the plane? Are they nervous about flying it?

Certainly, someone on the Board must have challenged the CEO, right? Apparently not.

This kind of passive behavior is not that of a functioning board. It is B-O-R-E-D behavior. In the middle of one of the company's most challenging moments in history, nobody, ostensibly, asked the CEO about the real story.

Why aren't the Board of directors, whether public or private companies, more engaged?

One reason may be that the popular and academic literature on leadership and transformation tends to ignore the Board. Perhaps that's because the Board's perception is not strategic; it's more of a rubber stamp. The presentations by executives get sanitized before they reach the Board, and its members don't challenge the executives. As a result, boards are not a

---

[3] A. Pasztor, D. Sider, and A. Sider. "Boeing Backs MAX Simulator Training in Reversal of Stance—WSJ," *The Wall Street Journal.* www.wsj.com/articles/boeing-recommends-fresh-max-simulator-training-11578423221?mod=searchresults&page=1&pos=9

[4] Baldanza, Interview.

[5] C. Woodyard. May 25, 2019. "On Autopilot: 'Pilots are Losing Their Basic Flying Skills,' Some Fear After Boeing 737 Max Crashes," *USA Today.* www.usa-today.com/story/news/2019/05/25/boeing-737-max-8-autopilot-automation-pilots-skills-flying-hours-safety/1219147001/

force for change. No company needs a board filled with folks there only for the money and the esprit de corps at the dinner before the day of meetings. Board members should feel moved by the larger purpose of the organization. Joe Astrachan, who has served on 20 boards and is an Emeritus Professor of Management at Kennesaw State University and Family Business Fellow at Cornell University, puts it simply:

"You'll agree with me when I submit that there are good managers and bad managers," he said.

"Of course," I replied.

So, will you agree with me that there are good boards and bad boards?

A weak board stays complacent, never challenging the information that they're spoon-fed. On the other hand, a strong board includes members with the experience, knowledge, intelligence, and personality to get to the truth of what's going on behind what the CEO is telling them.[6] [See Table 5.1 Bored vs. Board for a list of distinctions between the two board personality types.] While boards don't set the organizational velocity (OV) strategy, members should provide the framework for it, actively seeking truth and holding the CEO accountable to the mindset that drives new growth. The Board can't be bored. They must be engaged.

 Truth Bomb: There are good boards, and there are bad boards.

Boards Can Handle the Truth

In most companies, the idea that the Board of directors makes important decisions during its meetings is a myth. Most decisions are made well in advance, the meeting a formality. Board presentations tend to be watered-down versions of the truth meant to pacify rather than engage. Yet, the

---

[6] Astrachan, Interview.

Table 5.1 Bored vs. Board

Bored	Board
Manage risks	Ensures necessary risks are taken
Rely on previous experience	Continual learning/engaging
Compensation structure "consistent with industry"	Compensation structure encourages correct firm-specific behaviors
Extensive interaction with other Board members	Extensive interaction with top management team, customers, and industry experts
Highly cleansed presentations	Thought provoking presentations
Back-to-back presentations at meetings	Performance and committee reporting done in pre-reads. Issues and opportunities requiring debate and discussion dominate agenda
No participation in strategy creation	Guide culture and frame (not set) strategy
Relies on research provided from management	Does their own research
Pre-meeting board dinners, heavy on wine, light on substance.	Board dinners include management team paired with board members; pre-meeting breakfast to review notes from dinner and action plan for meeting
Management dictates agenda	Board dictates agenda
"Back 'em or sack 'em"	Challenge, encourage, coach
Shareholder focus	Stake holder focus
Nose in, hands out	Heart, gut and nose in, hands out
Seek prestige and compensation—need to be there	Seek fulfillment—want to be there
Providing good answers	Asking good questions
Homogeneous backgrounds	Heterogeneous backgrounds
Tech aware	Tech-savvy
Focus on whether the company is doing things right	Focus on whether the company is doing right things
Encourage innovation	Demand innovatio—set the tone with the CEO by providing permission to innovate (reflected in risk tolerance, KPI's and compensation)

Board's purpose is not merely to rubberstamp the carefully crafted report but to think aggressively about the future. Was COVID-19 on the full agenda of the January 2020 board meeting of any publicly traded companies? What about disruptive technology?

If not, that is a red flag. Or maybe, the white flag of surrender.

The sanitation of presentations to the top management team or the Board is a cliché. Often the issue is a misalignment of objectives.

The presentation creators see the chance to communicate the opportunity or threat that they see in the market and propose a course of action to the group that holds the purse strings. At the same time, the management layer(s) between the creators of the presentations and the decision makers want to make progress as well. However, they also despise ruffling feathers. Their fear of upsetting the apple cart, or looking stupid, wins out. The goal is to get out of the meeting unscathed. The last thing anyone wants to be asked is a question that they can't answer; hence, presentations are carefully crafted to avoid any danger zones. Too often, managers are ruled by fear: "What will the Board think of me? What will happen to my career if they decide to 'kill the messenger?'" When leaders don't speak up, insights perish, and opportunities are lost.

"I'd just completed redoing a deck for an executive meeting that was simply painful," a senior vice president recently said to me, "because with every iteration, we had to dumb down the message to the point where the final message at the meeting ended up being, 'We're good. We don't need to do anything.'" Of course, the truth was quite the opposite.

The following hypothetical situation illustrates how the sanitation process happens over months, sometimes years. The only part of this example not based in reality is the number of revisions. Since these presentations address more than one topic, there are typically many more than four revisions.

Original

These three market factors have coalesced over the last 18 months, negatively impacting margins in the Widget Division but creating an opportunity for Acme Corp to create a substantial new revenue stream. We're proposing three pilots addressing this opportunity with different value propositions. We need $50k for each pilot and a team of 12 people for nine months.

First Revision

These three market factors have coalesced over the last 18 months, creating an opportunity for Acme Corp to create a substantial new revenue stream. We propose a pilot project addressing this opportunity. We need $50k and a team of four people for six months.

Second Revision

These three market factors have coalesced over the last 18 months, creating an opportunity for Acme Corp to create a substantial new revenue stream. We are conducting additional customer research to validate the opportunity. If the research confirms the opportunity, we will come back to you next quarter with a proposal to pilot a solution.

Third Revision

These three market factors have coalesced over the last 18 months. The market changes create a potential new revenue opportunity for Acme Corp. We're working with McBain to do a "deep dive" on this opportunity.

Fourth Revision

We've been following changes in these three market factors that may impact the Widget Division. As we learn more, we will keep the Board updated.

So how does change happen at established companies if all the aspiring top managers are walking on eggshells? They gradually establish a consensus while sand slips through the hourglass. If their sanitized proposal gets some positive comments, the manager will start there—and only then see if they can build consensus one decision maker at a time. Here's the rub—like any material, ideas that are too polished cannot be grasped and simply slip through one's fingers.

 Gold Nugget: Like any material, ideas that are too polished cannot be grasped and simply slip through one's fingers.

In a conversation with a board member of a multi-billion-dollar global company, he said, "My experience with corporate boards is if the board chair and the CEO have a symbiotic kind of positive relationship, the business really moves forward. If the board chair is a placeholder, then we're going through the motions to check the boxes at the board meetings and the CEO is on a different path doing his or her thing."

Trust is a vital topic as it relates to the CEO-Chair relationship. The key is to create the opportunity for debate; if there's not an ability to have that debate, the Board is B-O-R-E-D. While at UPS, I recall leaving a meeting with a colleague who told me something they were thinking about during the session but never said out loud. The idea vaporized into the ether, never to return. When board members are silent, the opportunity to move the organization forward stalls. However, when board members are encouraged to speak from intuition and experience, they create new angles of thinking for the organization. It's far more productive than simply reading a highly polished 500-page report.

 Gold Nugget: It's the act of verbalizing from intuition and experience that board members create new angles of thinking.

The goal is more time for engaging the ideas from the report—and less time being presented to. But, again, that requires mutual trust, an environment where honest assessment is welcomed. The question, "Where do we want to be?" followed by a robust and open discussion is expected of companies built to last forever. In times of rapid change, the top management team must continually engage the Board to move rapidly. Just because a company views itself as a Forever Company doesn't mean it has forever to stay relevant.

You Don't Have Forever

Blockbuster wrongly thought that it had forever.

In 1993, six years after Wayne Huizenga invested in Blockbuster and became its second CEO, the company bought up local and regional video store chains, growing the chain significantly to 3,600 stores. When the low-hanging fruit was gone, Huizenga sold to Viacom for $8.4Bin 1994. Viacom then brought in senior executives from Walmart and 7-Eleven to help them make sense of customer data. On the surface, they did all the right things, leveraging technology to get insights from what would soon be referred to as "Big Data." The team drove improvements to both the top and bottom lines.

Blockbuster became the master of retail during this Gold era, cramming store shelves with candy, toys, and other quick-pick merchandise. John Antioco, CEO from 1997 to 2007, was a retail genius and that permeated every corner of the organization, which viewed itself as quintessentially retail—not a movie provider.

By 2004 they had 9,000 stores worldwide, revenues of $5.9 billion, and a market cap of $5.0 billion. Then the bottom dropped out as premium TV channels and Netflix offered from-the-sofa access to movies. As I mentioned in chapter 2, Blockbuster's retail bias—or its "marketing myopia"—was no different than Kodak seeing itself as a film company rather than a capturing-memories company and Borden seeing itself as a dairy company rather than a milk products company. (We see signs of this today as well. Wells Fargo seeing itself as a bank, leaves the company vulnerable to fintech leaders like Coinbase, Robinhood, and Lemonade.)

At some point, one would think the Board would see the competition and challenge the business model. Blockbuster had a 12-year head start on Netflix and even passed up a chance to buy Netflix for $50 million in 2001 (Netflix was valued at $270 billion in December 2021). But the management team didn't see the threat, or possibly they didn't know what they needed to do. They might have thought they would be around forever without tweaking their strategy. Boldly stepping out of consensus, CEO John Antioco launched an online-based DVD-by-mail business in 2006. In 2012, Blockbuster prepared to launch a streaming service (when Netflix's market cap was a mere $6 billion).

However, according to a former Blockbuster CMO, the Board was so retail-focused that its members viewed embracing online as a threat to Blockbuster's future; they thought it would cannibalize foot traffic. It was the ultimate irony. The Board at this moment couldn't check the management team's bias because they had the same bias! On top of that, the addition of activist board directors led by Carl Icahn created a short-term bias that made longer-term changes untenable.

The demise of Blockbuster yielded many lessons, but one lesson rarely discussed is the need for diversity on the Board. A lack of diversity renders a board ineffective. You might as well have cardboard cutouts of the board members. The same rich experience that makes board members so valuable is the same experience that can create a bias that hinders OV. That is if all have similar experiences. Consequently, the essential component of change—a challenge of the status quo—doesn't occur.

If board members think they have forever but don't embrace a "Forever Company" philosophy, then management efforts to adapt to market changes are dead on arrival. The future is created every day, and existing positions must be continually updated and revised. Board members must challenge the management team to fight the tendency to focus on what you sell versus the value you provide.

Board members must speak up; they have to challenge. Not because they don't trust the CEO, but because they do.

> Gold Nugget: Board members must speak up; they have to challenge. Not because they don't trust the CEO, but because they do.

Embracing Risk

For an organization to embrace the OV mindset and framework, so must its Board. OV is not a project. It's not something to champion for a certain period of time. It's a way of life. It's a way of living differently in the years of the Fourth Industrial Revolution. And increasingly, it's not an optional life choice.

One director recently lamented to me about his board meetings being so quick and efficient that "you can almost do it as a recording; you don't even need to be there." This director proposed dividing up board members and executive team members into smaller groups and giving them three questions to discuss so they could get underneath the surface information they heard. Unfortunately, the idea was shut down with a terse, "That's not the way we do it."

A board with experienced members and an archaic process can create a default cultural mindset that assumes the company can apply what worked in the past to fundamentally new threats or opportunities. One director told me about an annual board meeting that spends 40 percent of the agenda reviewing all of the risks in the business—from financial risk to safety risk to insurance risk. The one risk rarely on the agenda is the risk of disruption. Board meeting agendas tend to focus on what has happened or what is happening, not what may happen.

One of the better ways to ensure a board is facing disruption risk head-on is to devote one board member to disruption risk. This helps ensure that the Board is creating the agenda and challenging management, not the other way around. The Board can't expect the leadership to accept some reasoned risk to move with OV if they are unwilling to do the same.

 Gold Nugget: Ensure the Board is facing disruption risk head-on by devoting one board member to focus on this area.

Be aware that lawyers can be a significant roadblock. Legal counsel on the Board or at meetings will want to shut down the discussion of disruption. Paradoxically, it's legally worse to discuss disruption and do nothing about it than never to discuss it in the first place. If the Board doesn't discuss it, there may be less legal liability.

Give Permission

As I have stated, OV first requires a change in mindset followed by a change in operations. The Board encourages a mindset change when it gives the CEO permission to do things differently. Then, the CEO turns around and gives senior managers the same permission to do the following:

- Not be perfect
- Learn quickly and iteratively
- Take reasoned risks
- Make decisions
- Provide the same permissions all the way to the front lines

Permission does not have to be specific. Perhaps the most helpful and important permission a board can give is simply releasing the CEO and the senior team to do what they need to do. It's encapsulated in one word, "Go." Obviously, this is not an allowance to go rogue, but the explicit permission to make decisions and take risks. It establishes a foundational layer of trust between a board and the management. During the pandemic, this kind of permission was even more critical, especially when everyone ran scared.

Ben Baldanza, the former CEO of Spirit Airlines, gave me this example:

> During the most formative changes at Spirit in the change of the business model, there were things we did that the Board could have said, "Don't do that." And they never did that. In fact, in 2010, [in] one of the most controversial things Spirit ever did ... we announced that we're going to charge for large carry-on bags ... And that went over like a lead balloon ... [The response was] so negative ... our Chairman and the Board didn't say, "Ben, you can't do that." They said, [something to the effect] "Make sure we're not in the country the day you announce this." They were willing to test what we believed in.[7]

This wasn't a rash decision. Ben and his team had the data to back the decision and a process for implementing the change. "And what we learned after the fact," said Ben, "was the private equity firm that owned the company at the time actually had bets within their group as to how many months we would do it before we pulled it back." Ten years afterward, the policy is still intact. And Spirit's airplanes are still full.

OV requires the rapid pressure testing of ideas outside the corporate bubble. The Board should be part of that external pressure testing, and the permission they give expedites it. Board members are selected for their outside viewpoint—from different industries, with various skill sets. It's this outside perspective that should be used to help question current reality. The essence of OV is its iterative process—ergo, observe, accept, and act. The Board should help with "observe," but they have even a

---

[7] Baldanza, Interview.

larger role with "accepting," because of the permission that they can provide the CEO creating the boundaries for decision making.

At the same time, board members must be able to conduct their own research, independent of what the management says is going to happen. Board members need to "logic check" assumptions and provide a framework for the CEO and her team. Whatever the risk or opportunity, there are always indicators boards can look at to ascertain if management's vision is rational. For example, economic trends, geo-political developments, new technology introductions.

It's the job of the Board to critically challenge the CEO and his or her leadership team. Not in an obnoxious way, of course. But the Board cannot simply presume that what the CEO and the sanitized presentation says is fully true. CEOs need the background, judgment, and expertise of the Board.

You Need a "4-Star General"

As I wrote in the chapter on leadership, OV requires a leader with the right mindset, someone willing to take informed risks. The Board is directly responsible for that hiring decision. Some of the most innovative companies over long periods of time are founder-led. That is, the entrepreneur who started the company and stayed at the helm for decades.

Mark Kvamme was on LinkedIn's Board when the company was faltering and brought in Jeff Weiner to run the company. "We had a lot of issues," said Mark, "and we brought in Jeff Weiner, who was not a founder but knew how to partner with Reid Hoffman and made LinkedIn what it is today."

The LinkedIn board took a risk on Weiner, who had never been a CEO before. In fact, Weiner had not even been the general manager of a large enterprise. Mark continues:

[Weiner] was Steven Semel's right-hand man, both at Warner Brothers and then at Yahoo, but we just saw something special in the guy. And so, the problem a lot of these companies have, I have found, is that they basically think about what the prototypical CEO should look like. That CEO is very good at managing the Board. That CEO's very good at managing investor relations. They're very good at structuring, doing all this other kind of fun stuff … they're more of a two-star general than a four-star general.[8] I mean, four-star generals are brilliant human beings. If you get up to four stars, you are innovative, you are a great manager, you are a great leader … a two-star general is kind of like a director of operations.

It's the Board's job to hire the four-star general, not the administratively minded operations leader who manages the Board so that the organization runs efficiently. The role of the Board is to allow the CEO to make mistakes. "If you don't allow the CEO to make mistakes, then [he or she] won't take chances," said Mark. Boards must allow for failure, as long as it's guided failure in the pursuit of a goal—with the expectation that the organization will learn, iterate, adapt, and move forward as a result.

 Gold Nugget: It's the Board's job to hire the four-star general.

One final note on hiring: integrity matters—always has, always will. McDonald's seemed to forget this perennial fact in the hiring of the beleaguered Steve Easterbrook. The systems and lines of communication internally must have been gummed up enough for the Board to have no clue of his relationships with subordinates.[9] Possibly, they overlooked his craziness because he was turning in one great financial performance after another. That his prior boss didn't know or chose not to categorize him with a gross negative disqualifier says volumes. Then the Board hired him; how? Yes, Steve Easterbrook was a Four-Star General, but integrity remains the core prerequisite of a leader.

---

[8] Kvamme, Interview.
[9] J. Kelly. August 26, 2020. "The Saga of McDonald's Fired CEO Is Heating Up With New Allegations," *Forbes*. www.forbes.com/sites/jackkelly/2020/08/26/the-probe-into-mcdonalds-fired-ceo-is-heating-up-with-new-allegations/

Holding the CEO Responsible

It's not the Board's job to set the strategy but to help the senior team realize their stated strategy. If OV is an agreed-upon way of operating the business, then the Board supports the approach through incentives. One board chairman had an under-nuanced philosophy about the CEO. "You either back 'em, or you sack 'em." That, of course, does little to facilitate OV. The Board not only needs to provide the permission to move with speed and agility but the framework and boundaries to go with it. If the CEO and top management team are always second-guessing how the Board will interpret their actions, it adds friction to the wheels. Simply put, if a board aspires to hire a CEO to change the organization's trajectory through OV, then the Board truly needs to give the senior team the freedom to do so. And that takes courage.

When Jeff Weiner was hired to run LinkedIn, his style was completely different from the prior CEO. Weiner was much more transparent. One of his first acts was to start a weekly company wide meeting in which he took questions. He was transparent in a way that was different in kind from the previous leader. Mark Kvamme says, "I actually sat in one of those meetings with other board members, and it made me so nervous because I thought, *Holy crap, he's saying everything. What happens if XYZ company hears about that?*"

An essential instrument of the Board is the skill of "indirect influencing." It's completely different from directing the CEO and their senior team on *what* to do. Indirect influence is a separate category of leadership not talked about in the textbooks. The Board indirectly influences the specific issues put on the agenda, asking good questions, and providing additional information not already sanitized in the board presentation. "A board can help prioritize management by basically giving them the freedom to ignore certain things," said Ben Baldanza. "You can only work on these four things, but you don't have to worry about this right now."[10] This is a form of indirect influence—giving freedom to the management team to say that it's okay not to get some things done because other things are more important.

---

[10] Baldanza, Interview.

Gold Nugget: The Board empowers management to move fast on priority actions by giving the freedom to ignore certain things.

Another form of indirect influence is how people are called on for comments or questions. A sophisticated and wise chair knows the opinions of each of their board members and can artfully manage the discussion by calling on people for analysis. This often preempts negative opinions or allows everyone to voice the negative opinions at the beginning of the debate. That way, they won't inhibit or deflate later conversations.

In theory, no CEO has carte blanche authority to run the company without thinking of what the Board thinks. The Board hires the CEO, can fire the CEO, and sets the CEO's compensation. Boards can't (or shouldn't) tell the CEO what to do but should tell them what they can't do. The CEO can seek individual input from board members in one-on-one conversations, but having the Board agree on what the CEO should do is dangerous.

Hiring and Firing

Regarding CEO evaluation and compensation, today's boards abdicate both responsibilities to third-party companies like Korn Ferry, a global organizational consulting firm. The consultant comes in to evaluate the CEO and establish the compensation structure. There's nothing wrong per se with an outside firm setting a compensation benchmark. Compensation consultants provide insight on how compensation, both fringe benefits and salaries, compares to the company's industry peer group. But evaluation and compensation are two distinct processes. The challenge with outsourcing the evaluation component is that firms like Korn Ferry want to be hired again. No consultant is going to rip on the CEO. That would obviate the engagement a year from now.

The good evaluation firms start with 360-degree reviews of the CEO and the Board, followed by detailed developmental reports. These reports are not critiques; they focus more on identifying weaknesses and strengths. They offer suggestions for capitalizing on strengths and plans to address shortcomings at the individual level (CEO and board member) and group level (Board and CEO top management team). They are worthwhile.

However, board members are still responsible for evaluating the CEO. If a third party is engaged, board members cannot simply accept the report and move on to the next agenda item. Board members need to debate CEO performance and invest time in these discussions. Insiders (i.e., the Board) cannot abdicate the responsibility for performance evaluation to outsiders (consulting firms like Korn Ferry), who will take the path of least resistance. That's true of evaluating the CEO, as well as the Board. It's impossible to assess the contribution of a board member without being in the room and experiencing the person's contribution first-hand.

There's no way an outside consultant can read a board transcript and make any substantive evaluation of the contribution of a board member. What happens with outside consultants and their soft reviews of the CEO also happens with their assessment of board members: "It's all good. No need to worry. Every board member is doing great! So here's our rubber stamp, in case the SEC ever comes calling."

If the evaluator is not in the boardroom, it's nearly impossible to conduct a proper evaluation of a board member.

 Truth Bomb: If you're not in the boardroom, you can't conduct a proper evaluation of a board member.

The Board shapes the organization's future with their choice of CEO and the influence they wield over the top management team selections; not just the right people, but the right category. A business luminary who had studied boards extensively explained that many accountants and lawyers tend to create friction for an OV firm while marketing, technology, and R&D people tend to have the opposite effect. Richard D'Aveni, The Bakal Professor of Strategy at the Dartmouth Tuck School of Business, recounted a specific example at General Motors:

> One of the problems of General Motors for years and years, decades, all the senior management came out of the Treasury Department in New York City, not from the factories. Naturally,

quality got ignored as the finance people will look at squeezing another dime out of it, meaning the organization machine, versus the people and the plant.

The importance of selecting the right people extends to the Board of Directors itself.

Selecting for Impact

The future view of an organization is compromised if the Board is full of executives in the twilight of their careers. Not every executive in their waning years has stopped growing, of course. Imagine rejecting Peter Drucker for your Board because of age. Drucker was more relevant at 90 years old than most executives at 50.

However, the Board's composition should represent the organization's strategic needs, transforming itself to become more tech-savvy. Research conducted by MIT in 2019 revealed that organizations with digitally savvy boards outperformed their less-sophisticated peers. Unfortunately, the ongoing challenge for boards is the lack of tech-savvy among its members, a third of whom admit to not having learned about innovation.[11]

A digitally savvy Board is comprised of members with an enterprise-level understanding of current technologies such as AI and Big Data. In addition, they are familiar with digital processes and platforms that enable new business models, an improved customer experience, and more efficient operations. This digital savviness is often a consequence of one of two activities: time spent, either as a board member or a senior executive, in a high-clock-speed industry (where business models change quickly, such as software or telecom), or having an executive role with a strong technology component. Researchers at MIT found that it takes three digitally savvy members to have a statistically significant impact. In fact, companies with three or more digitally savvy directors had 17 percent higher profit margins than those with two or fewer, 38 percent

---

[11]   P. Weill, T. Apel, S.L. Woerner, and J.S. Banner. 2019. "It Pays to have a Digitally Savvy Board," *MIT Sloan Management Review* 60, no. 3.

higher revenue growth, 34 percent higher return on assets, and 34 percent higher market cap growth.[12]

Filling a tech void on a board might mean reaching outside the industry. This is preferable to only including academics and professionals from the industry. If you can't build tech-savviness from within, it might be necessary to hire board members solely for their tech expertise. You simply can't wait for a board member to get up-to-speed (think the so-called 10,000-hour rule: 3.5 years at 8hrs/day)—the organization will lag behind.

The primary characteristic you want in a board member is expertise born from experience. Companies appoint a director to their Board primarily for their experience. They have an intuitive feel for the industry. The industry and business function to which they have dedicated their career is second nature. The Board often deals with complex situations where many factors need to be weighed simultaneously. This is where board members show their worth. They can reach back into their intuition to frame issues facing the firm.

 Gold Nugget: Board members show their worth when they reach back into their intuition to frame issues facing the firm.

Boards need directors who have invested the necessary time and effort in digital opportunities to intuitively connect the dots between what they know and the current situation in front of them. Firms that don't have this capability on their Board of directors will have to face only one uncertainty: how long it takes them to go bankrupt. They must have all the three qualities that comprise the Disruptors Trifecta, which I discussed in chapter 4: smart, knowledgeable, and technologically fluent.

Don't be overly concerned that your board members have so-called "skin in the game"; that can send a wrong signal. It indulges them. It's critical that the Board is filled with those who aspire to make an impact, who *want* to be there and don't *need* to be there.

Don't fill the Board with former CEOs. In my research, board members who have been CEOs come in two flavors. One is the former CEO,

---

who views themselves as better equipped to be the CEO than the current one. That type of board member will pick away at the current CEO and stick their nose into areas reserved for senior management. The other is the empathetic former CEO board member who thinks, "This Board is a bunch of jerks. My role is to be the CEO's cheerleader." A better approach is to limit or rule out altogether former CEOs as board members. Or perhaps only recruit those who were CEOs for a short time and have participated in at least five other boards before being evaluated by yours. In the past, companies sought out directors who had a successful history of building companies. The thinking was that such directors would contribute with their experience. "That doesn't work so well going forward now," says Richard Manoogian, Chairman Emeritus of Masco and former Ford Motor Company board director, "that's because in the Fourth Industrial Revolution, what worked even five years ago won't work in the present." Instead, Manoogian recommends putting people on the Board who are still running something and dealing with "all the things we didn't even worry about ten years ago."[13]

Velocity Fabric

OV is not an initiative for a certain period of time. It's not an 8-step system. There is no hiring an outside consulting firm to implement OV as a project while the company goes on with its regular business. It is a deep conviction that arises from within an organization. It's what's underneath the surface, at the foundation, that will ensure a pervasive mindset change and put a corresponding framework in place. And that foundation is primarily built on the Board.

Board members must be in the battle, not just observers of the battle. Board members with an attitude of "It doesn't matter what happens as long as I can't be held to blame" need to be replaced.

---

[13] R. Manoogian. April 22, 2020. "Chairman Emeritus of Masco and Former Ford Motor Company Board Director." Interview by Alan Amling.

> Gold Nugget: Board members must be in the battle, not just observers of the battle.

OV tests the corporation's fundamentals—what we believe in, what we seek to achieve, what we reward, why we promote, how we talk to each other, and how we approach everything from information access to who receives decision-making authority to accept more risk.

A board first needs to understand the essence of OV, the "why" of it. The Board can then facilitate a structure that allows the company to operate with OV. Not just for growing the business, but for achieving the company's environmental and social goals. OV transcends profits. It is woven into the fabric of the community, and the Board provides the tools to make that happen. They exert direct and indirect influence with the issues they raise, the questions they ask, and the information they provide.

However, the key for any of these positive changes to take root—for OV to flourish—is to create an environment that doesn't lead to boardroom boredom.

What?

OV begins with the Board of Directors. Boards that see their role as merely keeping the firm out of trouble enable a path to irrelevancy.

So What?

Boards have the ultimate opportunity to challenge strategic direction and provide the permission senior leaders need to move with speed and agility. An OV leader must make strategic moves before they become obvious. Providing "air cover" for well-reasoned risk-taking allows leadership to test, learn, and grow at the pace of change.

Now What?

Transparency and engagement between the Board and the top management team before, during, and after board meetings must be standard practice. There must be complete trust between the Board and the management team for this to happen. If not, fix that first. Before all heads can be held high, some heads may have to roll.

CHAPTER 6

Extreme Trust

Trust is like the air we breathe—when it's present, nobody really notices. When it's absent, everyone notices.
—Warren Buffett

I played college football at a small Division III school called Lewis and Clark College in Portland, Oregon. I was a fullback, a non-heroic position with few opportunities to run the ball and even fewer chances to catch a pass. I was primarily a blocking back. My main responsibility was to block the meanest players on defense—the linebackers.

One of my favorite plays was the 22 Trap. It was my rare shot at running the ball. The guard would pull to trap the defensive tackle, the quarterback handed me the ball, and I hit the hole for a couple of yards. Usually, the middle linebacker tackled me only a yard or two beyond the line of scrimmage. It was a short-yardage play to keep the defense honest, more than anything.

We played Pacific University in Oregon on a natural grass field during my senior year after a couple of weeks of heavy rain. At a small college in the wet and western parts of Oregon, keeping a natural grass field ready for play was impossible. At the start of the game, there was no grass in the middle of the field, and as the game progressed, the middle of the field went from dirt to sludge.

Near the end of the game, the quarterback called the 22 Trap and handed me the ball. Instead of being slammed by the middle linebacker just beyond the line of scrimmage, I saw daylight. My feet pedaled as fast as they could go toward the goal line. Maybe the word "pedaled" isn't quite right. I've never sunk in actual quicksand, but I've watched enough old movies to understand the sensation. That is what running that day felt like. I was in the center of the field where there was no grass. I could hardly pick up my feet as I slipped and then sunk into the mud, lunging forward. The cornerback and safety were gaining on me from the edges of the field, where there was still grass.

I never made it to the goal line. I was tackled by the safety with two yards to go.

The goal was so close but so far away. I couldn't get there fast enough, given the slog through the mire. Every time I felt the slogging that came from trying to push ahead with innovation at UPS, I recalled my one shot at goal-line glory as a fullback.

That so-close-but-so-far-away feeling would often rush back running the project approval gauntlet. It was not uncommon to hear something to the effect of, "Alan, your project was approved, but we don't have enough billing resources to do it. So, we're going to have to put it off." The UPS safety tackled me again just short of the goal line.

I always protested, "Whatever your one billing resource is going to cost, I guarantee you it's not as much money as what it cost for my entire team to spend months pulling all this together. Can't we figure out a way to solve the billing problem?"

Nope. Too many budgets, all under different managers who had different metrics. When policy and bureaucracy get in the way of common sense, it stymies initiative and creates an environment of mistrust—in the system and each other.

This slogging, pushing hard to move incrementally forward simply slows innovation in a legacy company and ultimately drags down organizational velocity (OV). To switch metaphors, friction caused by a lack of trust throws sand into the velocity gears desperately needed by companies struggling to keep up with the startups of the Fourth Industrial Revolution.

Many organizations would say they have a culture of trust. But, it's a rare executive who would admit, "We're not good at trusting each other." For most, it's about chest-thumping and lip service. The executives all attend the same seminars and webinars, and read the same books on how trust creates culture; and yet, the Dilbert cartoonist has made a career satirizing trust in big corporations.

Processes that favor control over autonomy are one manifestation of mistrust, but examples come in many forms. For example, it shows up in how open and honest executives are in meetings, how much spending authority is granted, and how firms utilize consultants, to name a few. OV requires the practice of trust, not the statement or lip service of trust. You can't have velocity without it.

In the old model, trust is (supposedly) earned and meted out slowly over time: "Be a loyal and obedient employee, and we will gradually grant you more authority and responsibility." In the new model, trust is given. Access to data, spending authority, and other "control" elements are immediately handed to employees when they arrive to work the first day. Of course, this doesn't mean the keys to the kingdom are given to a new hire on day one, but it does mean that the new relationship begins with trust, and the employee deepens your trust (or not) through actions over time.

While this caveat might sound like "earning your trust," there is one key difference: by starting with trust as a rule, an organization takes its biases out of the equation and creates the opportunity for everyone to contribute at a faster pace. This enables OV.

I recently met with a former colleague now at Amazon, who recounted the first time she needed to access information at Amazon. She was able to access all the information she needed to complete her analysis, something she had never experienced in her past companies. In fact, she thought they had made a mistake and mistakenly given her too much access to data. "It blew my mind," she said, "I kind of stuttered a little bit. I was like, so what you're saying is anybody at Amazon can access that data? No wonder your [data project] would work; otherwise, we would all be standing in line like the DMV (Department of Motor Vehicles) to get information." Trust is given at Amazon. They hire for it. It manifests itself in hundreds of invisible ways every day, including allowing a new employee to quickly gain the information she needs to observe, accept, and act with speed and agility.

I've argued throughout this book about the existential importance of learning quickly. A company's survival depends on it. An organization can learn more rapidly than its competitors when its people trust one another wholly and implicitly. Trust is foundational to learning and is reflected in everything that an organization does. While there should be guidance with goals and parameters, employees cannot be bogged down by process (which reveals a fundamental lack of trust). Instead, they must be able to act, learn, and react to real-time information. Trust oils the joints of innovation in a company.

 Gold Nugget: The new paradigm is "Trust is Given." There is no velocity without it.

Invisible Asset

Trust, as everyone knows, is fundamental. Without trust, employees experience more stress, higher burnout, and less energy at work. A study in *Harvard Business Review* compared people at low-trust companies with people at high-trust companies. Not surprisingly, at high-trust companies there is 74 percent less stress, 106 percent more energy at work, 50 percent higher productivity, 13 percent fewer sick days, 76 percent more engagement, 29 percent more satisfaction with their lives, and 40 percent less burnout.[1]

Trust is invisible; there is no line item for it on a balance sheet. But its presence, or absence, is felt. Trust is like the wind, casting invisible seeds into every field of an organization. How organizations observe, accept, and act on threats and opportunities (the very definition of OV) is essentially a function of trust, manifesting in both high- and low-profile situations.

 Gold Nugget: Trust is like the wind, casting invisible seeds into every field of an organization.

Let's take, for example, the situation of an executive who is in a staff meeting and faced with an operations issue that could be detrimental to the company. He or she thinks, *I don't want to raise a red flag. What will my boss and colleagues think of me? If I'm right, then I'm Gold, but if I'm not ...* This scenario plays out every day in corporate meetings across the world. The first idea is usually not the best one. A problem revealed invites solutions, and people are eager to come up with ideas

---

[1] P.J. Zak. 2017. "The Neuroscience of Trust," *Harvard Business Review* 95, no. 1.

to fix it. In addition, as ideas are surfaced, everyone present may gain a different perspective that enables a better outcome. But if there's no trust among the team, the winnowed idea is never given a chance for a better result.

 Truth Bomb: A problem revealed invites solutions.

Let's say the executive is in another team meeting. He has an idea for his division that is a bit off the grid. It's based on current business trends and a view of the future that cannot be supported with facts (because it hasn't happened yet, the supporting data doesn't exist). Does the executive open his mouth and risk ridicule to put the idea on the table? He won't if there's no trust in the room. Ideas unexpressed become corporate cancer, eating away at the individual and depriving the firm of the very thing that can allow it to thrive in disruption.

Truth Bomb: Ideas unexpressed become corporate cancer, eating away at the individual and depriving the firm of the very thing that can allow it to thrive in disruption.

It's up to the CEO to set the tone for the transparent discussions that fuel an OV organization and lay the groundwork of trust that encourages transparency. These discussions can then lead to actions that cascade through the organization.

Here are two contrasting stories that exemplify the invisible power of trust. Before UPS went public, we had an old-school UPS operator who worked himself up to the CEO role. His name was Jim Kelly. When presenting to Jim and his staff, I was told to pause when someone asked a question and let the discussion unfold. It was always energizing. When I touched on a controversial point, invariably someone would raise their hand and the staff would actively debate back and forth. The CEO would listen. Sometimes he would jump in, make a statement, and I would move on. Other times he would just let the discussion play out. We were living our culture and hitting on all cylinders.

The last time I presented to the then-present CEO and his staff, the level of trust was night and day different. My marching orders for those meetings were, "Your only audience is the CEO. Don't move to the next slide until he turns the page. If he turns the page while you're still talking, move on." This leader had a career of accomplishment at UPS, but he was not an OV leader. The stone silence of his executive team was proof positive of a lack of trust and openness. Yet, you could see the ideas churning in their heads through their smiles and grimaces. One of those ideas could have been a difference-maker, like money in the bank that will never be spent.

Ric Fulop is the founder and CEO of Desktop Metal, a cutting-edge designer, manufacturer, and marketer of AM systems. Ric told me that the key to his company's OV success is its commitment to encouraging a free flow of ideas.

"Our culture is very forgiving," Fulop said. "We try a lot of things that don't end up working out, and there are no repercussions. No one's fired for making a mistake. We obviously don't like making mistakes, but we are open-minded. Sometimes companies are too focused on being focused that they are disadvantaged. It starts with ideas that didn't exist before." Organizations built on trust, like Desktop Metal, see crazy ideas become crazy successful.

 Gold Nugget: Organizations built on trust see crazy ideas become crazy successful.

While trust is given, it is never taken for granted. Honesty, integrity, following through, being at your best when your best is needed; all these characteristics remain cornerstones of any organization. Shopify CEO Tobi Lutke calls it charging the trust battery. He uses the analogy of a cell phone battery. If your phone is 80 percent charged, you're not thinking about your phone a lot. However, if you're on low battery mode, that's all you can think about.[2] Charging your trust battery through your everyday

---

[2] T. Lutke. December 16, 2020. "The Observer Effect – Tobi Lütke," Interview by Shane Parrish, *The Knowledge Project*. www.theobservereffect.org/tobi.html#trustbattery

actions is critical to OV, allowing the autonomy to focus on what's essential and not what should be table stakes. If anyone on your team runs their trust battery dry, fire them immediately, they're cancer.

The Flow of Trust

As I mentioned previously, organizations are gummed up by control mechanisms; low spending and decision-making authority, tedious and multi-tiered access to information, and Groundhog Day approval committees taking months or more to reach a decision. All organizations need proper governance, but a high level of control within rigid hierarchies indicates a lack of trust. Ask yourself why the spending authority for similar levels of responsibility across similar organizations varies greatly. You'll find that it's primarily about the level of trust. Trust in the individual. Trust in the process. Trust in the organization, your partners, and your customers.

During the COVID-19 pandemic, some companies installed tracking software on employee computers with employees working from home. Had employees thought to check the updates to their corporate laptop, they would have discovered all sorts of monitoring software, including software that takes screenshots of an employee's monitor at random intervals. Other software tracked keystrokes. It was the equivalent of an in-office desk check. Were these indicators of trust or suspicion between employee and employer? The answer depends on how much organizational trust the company has built up with its employees. Mac Quartarone, an organizational psychologist, said, "If you have a lot of trust, then you probably expect that the organization is just trying to do the right thing. If you don't have a lot of trust, then you're going to assume that they're trying to fire you or trying to find people that they need to fire."[3]

It is patently obvious, but if an organization wants to play in the green fields of the Fourth Industrial Revolution, then the practice of trust (not the statement of trust) is foundational. Employees looking over their

---

[3] S. Morrison. 2020. "Just Because You're Working from Home Doesn't Mean your Boss Isn't Watching You," *Vox*. www.vox.com/recode/2020/4/2/21195584/coronavirus-remote-work-from-home-employee-monitoring

shoulders are not looking ahead. Lack of trust creates inertia. It also gives rise to a bureaucratic tug-of-war that drains energy and squelches initiative. Employees are forced to endure loops of multiple approvals before they get an answer. Budgets are restricted without cause. And the company limits employee access to the data they need to make good decisions.

 Gold Nugget: Employees looking over their shoulders are not looking ahead.

The tug-of-war is between control and autonomy. As companies get larger, executives install bureaucratic fences to control spending and limit access to data. These measures of control stem from a lack of trust. In a startup, the CEO, the two programmers, the half-time marketing person, and the one sales rep pretty much work in the same room with access to everyone else's information. There's little need for extensive controls. As an organization grows, so does the sheer amount of data, with departments instead of individuals utilizing various kinds of information. Trust can no longer be assumed. It needs to be managed.

I'm not criticizing financial and data controls—and all other organizational rules necessary for smooth functioning. These don't necessarily indicate a lack of trust. That happens when the leader of an organization upholds the value of trust and then acts in ways that belie the trust he purports to cherish. This kind of behavior is more sand in the gears of OV. The leader loses credibility, and so does the company.

Walking the Talk

Many are the ways in which leaders talk one kind of trust game but play another. One of the most common is allowing executives to throw FUD (Fear, Uncertainty, and Doubt) in committee meetings, delaying or killing projects without providing alternatives that move the firm forward. Poking holes in projects to test for weaknesses is extremely valuable and expected at OV companies. But only when it's done in the spirit of evolving the idea forward. At Amazon, they have a term for the FUD throwers, "blockers." An Amazon executive told me in no uncertain terms, "You don't want to be a blocker."

Another demoralizing practice sends managers to a special team to access sensitive information they need to do their job. In an age in which data is the currency of work, this signals a fundamental lack of trust in the people who best understand the data. More examples are shown in Table 6.1.

Table 6.1 Thirteen ways leaders lie about trust

	Thirteen ways leaders lie about trust
1	Allowing executives to throw FUD (fear, uncertainty, and doubt) in committee meetings, delaying or killing projects without providing alternatives that move the firm forward.
2	Creating onerous processes for employees to access the critical information required to do their job.
3	Establishing low spending thresholds for management.
4	Doing "Desk checks".
5	Tabling controversial topics at executive meetings to be discussed with a smaller audience "Behind closed doors."
6	Allowing the "Water cooler talk" to become the primary source of company information.
7	Thwarting respectful disagreement and discussion in staff meetings.
8	Establishing austerity measures to get the company through a tough patch and then holding a meeting at some umbrella drink resort.
9	Delegating responsibility without providing commensurate authority.
10	Making decisions in a vacuum.
11	Playing the blame game.
12	Agreeing to a decision in a mesting and then actively under-mining that decision, even with a casual comment.
13	Promises not kept.

OV binds organizations together. One of my colleagues at the University of Tennessee, Kate Vitasek, has championed a revolutionary method of developing and managing logistics contracts called vested outsourcing (VO). Contracts are typically drawn up to protect both parties. They keep the other guy honest. VO contracts are more like a binding covenant between the two parties. Each is vested in the success of the other, sharing both the upside and downside of the relationship. P&G, for example, created a facility management relationship with Jones Lang LaSalle (JLL) that tied the service provider's profitability to the latter's ability to drive success against jointly defined business outcomes. The relationship led to a decade-long streak of JLL winning "supplier of the year" honors from P&G.[4]

The foundation of any VO agreement is trust. If there is not a sufficient level of trust between organizations, a vested relationship is not possible. Kate requires that both parties complete a Compatibility and Trust Assessment. If there are significant gaps in any of the trust elements, they must be addressed before she engages in the project. Kate knows that mutual relationships not built on a bedrock of trust cannot succeed.

Challenge Culture

One of the quickest ways a CEO can judge whether they are leading a culture of trust is to ask a series of basic questions that function as a trust barometer:

> Is there spirited debate in my staff meetings?
> Are people challenging each other?
> Are people challenging me?
> Are ideas getting acted on with urgency once the decision has been made?

If the answers are mostly "No's," the CEO doesn't turn around and implement trust initiatives. He or she looks inward. When the CEO acts in an OV way, exhibits humility, and asks questions, people will respond. They will want to talk and engage in spirited debate. Their leader has given them permission. In the Hollywood hero version of leadership, the CEO needs to know exactly what to do in every situation. They need to

---

[4] K. Vitasek. June 13, 2016. "Procter & Gamble, TD Bank: Vested Outsourcing Success Stories," *Facilitiesnet*. www.facilitiesnet.com/outsourcing/article/Procter-amp-Gamble-TD-Bank-Vested-Outsourcing-Success-Stories--16660

be infallible. They believe, "People will follow me if I exude the confidence that can only come from knowing everything."

That's narcissism, not leadership. Its motivation is power, a simplistic mindset that will only isolate the CEO and create silos in the company. It's simply not effective in a complex, technological, and data-driven environment. The CEO must provide conviction around the "what" and the "why" but there must be vigorous debate around the "how." And it starts with the CEO and how he or she interacts with the senior team.

> Gold Nugget: The CEO must provide conviction around the "what" and the "why" but there must be vigorous debate around the "how."

The lieutenants learn how to act from watching the CEO, not reading the policy book. CEOs create a culture by what they do. They walk the talk. When their actions are congruent with their words, they will foster trust and build up the culture.

If a CEO wants to create an organization with speed and agility, the very first thing they must do is *demonstrate* trust.

The Virtuous Cycle of Trust

Corporate trust is two-way: employees trust the organization's purpose and its leaders trust the people to pursue that purpose. Success happens when many people go above and beyond the call of duty to pursue a shared objective—not because they have to but because they want to. They're motivated. They want to achieve the objective: for themselves, their colleagues, and for all the stakeholders whose lives will be improved if the particular goal is accomplished.

A virtuous circle is created as an organization is transparent in the what, why, and how of the company. Much has been written about the "why" with the rationale that people will commit to an organization when they understand its purpose. But it's only when people internalize the purpose that they can move mountains. Knowing about the need to "take the hill" does not give soldiers the *will* to take the hill.

Gold Nugget: Create a virtuous circle in your organization by being transparent about the what, why, and how.

The "why" must be deeply internalized by everyone and communicated over and over through a clear and compelling narrative. Over time this "what" and "why" (narrative = mission, purpose, and values) become the culture of the organization.

Muscles provide strength, and trust is the tendon that attaches bone to muscle. You cannot have a strong organizational culture without trust. In a strong culture, employees have buy-in; they have faith that the leadership will act in a certain way. An employee in a strong culture thinks, "Who I am as a person is what the company wants. There is a match here." That mindset governs an employee's thoughts and actions.

Desktop Metal CEO Ric Fulop describes the difference between hiring "missionaries" and "mercenaries." "You have two types of people: missionaries and mercenaries. You want to have missionaries working in a startup environment because you will go through ups and downs or difficult times. You want people who eat, breathe, sleep the type of business we're in."[5] Legacy organizations who want to create OV need to generate a missionary mindset. The more workers believe and trust in the "why" of the organization, the more you can trust them with your organization's work.

 Gold Nugget: You want missionaries in your business who eat, breathe, and sleep the type of business you're in.

Culture, of course, is about the what and the why, but it is also about the how. The formula is this: (What + Why) × How = Culture. This chapter on trust sets up chapter 7, which is about the "how." The "how" is constantly improved and adjusted based on the current business context and new information. Employees must be able to trust management's intentions, that the senior team will act within the framework of the culture, even if the world falls apart. Trust is the glue of culture and it is quite

---

[5] Fulop, Interview.

easily weakened. Like with a spouse, switching metaphors, even a small behavior, can open a window in which trust is allowed to evaporate. If enough windows are opened, the relationship becomes at risk.

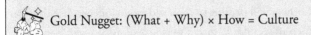 Gold Nugget: (What + Why) × How = Culture

Trust is realized through shared experiences of executing the "how" to accomplish the "what" (or not). Note the word *realized.* As discussed earlier, trust is given and then reinforced through repeated experiences. When trust is high, autonomy is high, and control is low. When trust is low, then control goes up, and autonomy goes down. This trust is one source of the Founders Advantage, the secret sauce enabling rapid growth. Founders of startups are typically tight-knit groups that know and trust each other and are motivated by a joint mission. Startups nearly always move with speed and agility. As businesses become large and trust based on personal interaction becomes more difficult, control mechanisms are put in to "manage" the work. Incumbent organizations must fight this tendency by creating new structures such as small autonomous teams to recapture the Founders Advantage. Autonomy based on trust is what creates OV.

How Trust Is Enabled

The COVID-19 pandemic exposed an eternal truth about organizational change. When the stock market collapsed and the shelter in place orders came down, suddenly companies that had been glacially slow to join the digital revolution were using Zoom as if they were digital natives. Pain is often the only way to change. There was no choice but to change! Learn and adapt ... or die. Companies didn't waste untold hours concocting new ways to control their employees; they started to experiment with online communication. They started pushing decision making to the people closest to the customer. And while the digital tools and certainly the more agile philosophy had been available to them for years, they didn't do it because they didn't have to do it. It took a gun to their head.

Absent of an external draconian agent, organizations simply default to comfort. Unless, of course, their leader enables the change to happen. As

I wrote previously, only the CEO can give permission to move with OV. And only the board of directors can provide that power to the CEO. Most likely, after the collateral damage of the pandemic starts to be repaired, a few companies will take a cue from what happened and continue to innovate. Many others will default to their old behaviors because this way of business is uncomfortable. It forces senior leaders to learn new skills. It changes the hierarchy, where the digital natives start to supervise the digital immigrants. The power structure will change.

For most of my career at UPS, I tried to put myself in uncomfortable positions; in doing so, I probably worked myself down the corporate ladder more than I needed to. I took lateral positions in new ventures instead of waiting for the promotion for a more direct move up. I was always tempted, however, to wait and see. To stay put and be comfortable. It's almost impossible not to succumb to the comfort of what you know. We all want certainty. Taking risks can beat you down after a while. That's why employees need constant reinforcement from the top level of the company: "What you're doing is critically important. This is part of our mission. And the learning is in the failing." All this is part of the corporate narrative, the story that shapes behavior, implicit and explicit.

In the 1930s, UPS issued stock to its employees. The founder said, essentially, "Everyone should have an ownership stake, and we're going to be a company owned by managers and managed by owners." Everyone called each other partners; there was an esprit de corps—all of the people policies revolved around supporting that egalitarian vision. A significant portion of the management team's compensation was in bonus at the end of the year. The bonus calculation was straightforward. Fifteen percent of profits got distributed based on the individual's management level. Everyone knew that if one department did exceptionally well and another didn't, the bonus was the same. It was all about how UPS did as a whole.

That single principle created behaviors that eliminated friction. Instead of trying to optimize only what you controlled, your focus was bigger; what was best for the company. At times, managers would potentially inhibit the performance of their division to help out another division if asked. As a result, resources were not hoarded but flowed to the area of greatest need. It may seem counterintuitive that a business could achieve greater individual accountability through a group-based incentive. Wouldn't "slackers" get away with not pulling their weight? While that happened occasionally, UPS's promote-from-within policy developed managers with a strong work ethic. "Slackers" at UPS were rare as rocking horse manure which is why UPS was "the tightest ship in the shipping business" long before the incentive plan changed.

Unfortunately, this cohesive culture, founded on trust, began to unravel when UPS went public. Suddenly there was scrutiny from the shareholders: how could you pay this division their bonus when the team didn't hit its goals? Bonuses became based on metrics that individuals may have very little influence over. Managers became focused on the parts at the expense of the whole. That is friction. I immediately felt the impact. When I moved from the core package delivery company to run global marketing for the Logistics & Distribution division, I tried leveraging some of my long-standing relationships only to hear, "I'm sorry. I would like to help, Alan. I just can't."

Over time, organizations accumulate friction. As they become larger, more controls are put in to manage risk. Decision-making authority is centralized; information becomes siloed. Managing for process becomes more valued than managing for outcomes. As investors clamor for financial returns, organizations establish short-term metrics, creating friction for longer-term "Forever Company" initiatives. Their past decisions, however, limit their future choices. For example, many commitments to sustainability get curtailed during economic downturns. Similarly, companies get addicted to dividends and stock buybacks to satisfy the quarterly needs of investors. The unwillingness to unwind past choices in the face of environmental change is a significant cause of friction in organizations. Of course, this is true for private as well as public companies.

Gold Nugget: The unwillingness to unwind past choices in the face of environmental change is a significant cause of friction in organizations.

The Hope of Trust

In the mid-90s I was part of a cross-functional, special-assignment team looking at how the Internet was going to impact commerce and UPS. We plugged along at a deliberate pace until an article came out in a trade magazine claiming that FedEx was now "The Airline of the Internet."

This sat well with no one. No senior executive could countenance that FedEx had somehow outrun us. The executive over marketing and sales put his trust in our group and made changes that allowed OV to happen. He provided a healthy budget, pushed decision making to the edge, and created a direct line to him for the big decisions. He also provided "air cover" to prevent others from creating friction. We had unfettered access to the resources we needed and the permission to act. It was wonderful.

We developed an e-commerce strategy during a short period and created many of the core offerings that are still in place two decades later (albeit improved over time). Since then, of course, e-commerce has evolved from a fad to a global phenomenon, accounting for about 70 percent of UPS package volume in 2020.

Our progress, however, created jealousy and fear among some members of the IT group. In essence, we were given permission to go around IT. Working in e-commerce at the dawn of the Internet gave us a high profile within UPS with immediate financial impact and a fresh value for our customers. Quickly, however, there was a counter-movement within the company. The thinking was, "The e-commerce initiative must go through our strategic processes." It was the old "We're the government, and we're here to help." Not long after, spending on our initiative was curtailed, with new controls put in place. In essence, we reverted back to our Old Self: "I don't trust that you are going to spend the money wisely. You're not an IT person. I'm an IT person. I understand better. I should have the money, and then you can come to me with your project, and I will tell you the best way to do it because I understand IT."

And that's precisely how it went down. Our $8 million budget went to IT, and from that day forward, our e-commerce team lost control of our destiny. We had been corralled. The Wild West was over. Or, as Marine Colonel Howie Marotto put it, "Bureaucracy fights back."[6]

 Truth Bomb: Bureaucracy fights back.

While the story doesn't end well, this was a short run of OV at UPS. And it was exhilarating—the feeling of trust that comes from a friction-free, sludge-free path. This kind of trust is within the grasp of every organization, no matter how old or staid. Trust, the fuel for OV, is available to every firm. Give trust and get results. And, as with most corporate progress, it starts at the top.

What?

Trust is the foundation for OV.

So What?

Absent trust, barriers are put in place that will bring OV to a crawl. Roadblocks that reduce autonomy and increase control to "manage" the productivity of the firm. While leaders may be able to control performance with better tools, they risk being lapped by more nimble competitors acting with a sense of urgency.

Now What?

Start with trust. Don't hire anyone you don't trust implicitly from the start. Employees who break the trust bonds need to be dealt with professionally and swiftly; they are cancer to the organization. Read Table 6.1, "Thirteen Ways Leaders Lie about Trust." Are you doing any of these things? Recognize the delicate balance between autonomy and control and strive to operate with more autonomy when and where you can.

---

6   H. Marotto. October 28, 2018. "Colonel, Deputy Commander, 4th Marine Logistics Group." Interview by Alan Amling

CHAPTER 7

Be the Third Pig

Building an OV Organization

If you defer investing your time and energy until you see that you need to, chances are it will already be too late.

—Clayton Christensen

Do the right thing. Since I was young it's been ingrained in me, which makes doing the wrong thing feel so wrong.

While I was at UPS, one long-standing policy was, "We pay our bills promptly. We do this because it is right, because it is a good business practice, and because it strengthens our reputation and our credit rating." But in December of 2018, a vendor with whom I worked closely had a big payment due. My manager asked me to push the payment into 2019.

"I won't do it," I said. "It's against our policy."

"It is," he said, and I saw the pain on his face. He was a UPS veteran, loyal to its core culture and founding vision. "You're going to have to do it anyway. This is coming from above us."

I knew what he meant. The directive from the UPS leadership was part of a larger effort to drive results fast enough for Wall Street to recognize and reward. It went against everything in me.

Holding the payment was symptomatic of a seismic shift at UPS.

The company was founded in 1907 by Jim Casey, who, at the Plant Managers Conference in 1954, laid out UPS's ten-year vision "to act as the delivery department of retail stores … at rates lower than any other means of transportation." The following year, Jim Casey and his managers established the core principle which would undergird his vision: the employees who helped pioneer UPS would have ownership of the company.

This partnership philosophy helped fuel UPS's steady growth until 1999 when the company went public and started to make decisions that began undermining this foundational principle. Still prioritizing growth, UPS made a series of acquisitions to expand into supply chain solutions. The company also created a financial services division, UPS Capital. In theory, management still controlled the company, but appearances belied the reality. UPS had gone from a company owned by managers and managed by owners to a company that now had to defend its decisions to disconnected investors every quarter.

This was not a failure of integrity or good intention, both of which remained a vital part of the UPS culture. But it had forgotten the "you" in its long-retired slogan, "What can brown do for you?" Instead, it drove the company inward, serving the demands of its shareholders instead of optimizing employee and customer experience.

UPS had gone on the defensive, even as the digital economy began to reveal leaks in the company's competitive moat. Technology solutions exclusive to the large logistics companies that could afford the expensive and complex systems were now becoming available from the cloud to startups on a pay-by-the-drink basis. Everyone from multinational accounts to individual consumers was exerting more influence as they acquired the greatest source of power since the dawn of time, information.

UPS was on the proverbial horns of a dilemma it had created: how to answer to investors as it sought to transform the company.

In response, UPS brought in outside consultants and effectively isolated its most valuable asset—its employees—from its customers and each other. The consultants were heavily biased toward metrics that few people could impact directly. As discussed in chapter 6, the management profit-sharing program was discontinued, and UPS managers stopped referring to each other as "partners." The metrics driving the business reflected the loss of an esprit de corps among the managers. Only one metric, ultimately, mattered: Return on Invested Capital (ROIC). This pragmatic approach caused UPS to pull on the efficiency lever at the expense of exploring new revenue streams.

Reality is already unforgivingly complex, to which disruption adds truths not yet discovered that are equally if not more complex. You don't know what you don't know. And it's good to know that you don't know what you don't know. The problem with many established companies is that they have relied for decades on what they know—and fail to address what they don't know. Motorola, GE, Yahoo, and JC Penney were staffed with intelligent leaders who racked up substantial commercial success before and after their tenure. They came into these storied companies with biases they looked to confirm. Those biases left unchecked would hinder them and their companies simply because they worked against diversity of thought and discovery—a willingness to explore the unknown.

These dilemmas of disruption are remarkably persistent whether the firm is public, private, or family-owned. Overcoming internal biases and allocating precious resources to unproven opportunities, lower-margin products, or initially small customer segments does not happen without fierce debate, ever. However, through this uncomfortable debate and the acceptance stage of organizational velocity, resilience is created.

> ✳ Truth Bomb: Reality is already unforgivingly complex, to which disruption adds truths not yet discovered that are equally if not more complex.

Releasing Friction

UPS's situation in the early 2020s points to the difficulty of balancing what's great about a company while adapting to a new business context. A market bursting with pandemic-driven demand, capacity shortages, and new competitors. It's not for the weak of heart, but it can be done. As founder Jim Casey did in UPS's ascendant years, a strong leader will rally the company around a straightforward, compelling narrative and inspire change for everyone. This kind of change is not incremental. It requires a complete overhaul that first begins with a shift in mindset.

But, of course, a story is not enough. Organizations need a supporting structure that provides the best opportunity to win. Put the two together, and you have what I call an organizational velocity (OV) organization; it's the proverbial house of bricks that the forces of change can't blow down.

An OV organization understands and addresses two tendencies of human nature: our desire for change and our penchant to resist change. Our resistance, often stronger than our desire for change, creates friction. Unless the purpose is to create fire, friction generally rubs the wrong way. It restricts movement and retards progress. In an organization, resistance can manifest in many ways, including the hoarding of information. Information, obviously, is power. It's revolutionary. It changes everything. Its opposite is ignorance which breeds fear, failure, and the fear of failure. Want your organization to take off? Want to allow for persistent advantage? Reverse resistance by getting information flowing.

An OV organization despises ignorance. So it disseminates information rather than bottlenecking it. Internally, it opens the channels for information to flow by creating an open, agile and adaptable environment where people are encouraged to experiment without the fear of failure. Failed experiments are welcomed as learning experiences; which fosters faster change. It's a virtuous cycle.

An agile and open internal environment can also pragmatically and quickly shift in response to external changes. This requires a mind shift in leadership from command and control style (which increases friction) to sense and respond (which reduces friction). We tend to react to events in two ways. We either move toward or away from whatever happens, but naturally, we tend to be defensive. OV companies create an environment that changes this defensive mentality into an offensive mindset—open and curious.

Charles Koch, CEO of Koch Industries, proves that becoming OV is about attitude, not age. His creation of Market-Based Management (MBM) may be his greatest legacy. MBM has been Koch's overarching approach to value creation and capture across the Koch companies. This means that beyond culture, MBM also serves as a strategic roadmap to how they think and where they focus their resources. MBM is made up of eight guiding principles: integrity, stewardship and compliance, Principled Entrepreneurship, transformation, knowledge, humility, respect, and self-actualization.[1] This is not just words on paper at Koch; it's a way of life. Darin Dredge, a Director at Koch subsidiary Guardian Industries explained, "We don't acquire companies and try to turn them into Koch Industries. We buy companies like Georgia-Pacific, Guardian, and Infor, and use MBM to change the culture of those firms. This is because even with MBM, all companies under the Koch umbrella will have their own unique characteristics."[2] According to Darin, some of this is driven by industry, the history of the organization, and many other factors. Hence, they say all of the companies in the portfolio are powered by MBM, which Charles Koch regularly credits as the most important factor in the company's long-term success.

The Big Payoff of a Small Bets Strategy

Risk is both the dopamine and the beta-blocker of an organization. High risk, high reward is for high rollers. But most people aren't built with that kind of risk tolerance. The leaders in OV organizations understand this. They start to change culture with a strategy that gradually increases risk tolerance while also opening an organization to thinking outside the box. In efficiency-minded companies, the box is existing revenue models, and the energy of the organization is focused on optimizing what's in the box. But there's a much better approach to increasing revenue, what I call the small bets strategy.

The more efficient the firm, the harder it is to change processes and move assets in response to changes in the market. Without OV, more efficiency only slows the demise of an organization; it doesn't create its future. Efficiency streamlines an existing process, but it doesn't create new revenue streams. This is where small risks need to become a part of the overall strategy.

---

[1] C.G. Koch. 2007. *The Science of Success: How Market-Based Management Built the World's Largest Private Company.* John Wiley & Sons.
[2] Video interview with Darin Dredge, Director, Guardian Industries, October 05, 2020.

The most important data is that which hasn't been created yet. Small bets in the form of experiments, pilots, or proofs of concepts can help firms discover that data and accelerate their learning cycle. The strategy is based on the premise that outcomes are always unknown, especially where human behavior is involved. Being right in time is as important as being right in concept. By funding three projects, for example, taking three different paths to the same outcome, companies can get to the optimal solution more quickly. (I discussed this multi-pronged process, using small-bet pilots, in chapter three). Of course, that means you funded two projects that would end up being mothballed. For companies that prize efficiency, this method could seem like heresy until they realize they have been efficiently producing an inferior product. Their less efficient, small bets competitor has come up with something better. By testing multiple options, they have reached the best solution while cutting their time to market.

A small bets strategy does not originate in a conference room but from the OV process of continually and iteratively observing and accepting *before* acting. It's the serenity prayer applied to OV. Accept what you cannot change so you can change what you can. Acceptance ultimately leads to the right action. Multiple hypotheses are formed, and those hypotheses are tested simultaneously in "the real world." When a hypothesis proves true, then you act.

Importantly, the intent to act on a successful small bet must be established before any discovery begins. Companies can find themselves in pilot purgatory if they are just dipping their toe in the water of innovation. Without a commitment to learn, iterate, and act on outcomes, small bets tend to lack the involvement and support of the leaders that would need to implement them, and the learnings end up on the shelf.

> Gold Nugget: Organizations without a commitment to act on outcomes will find themselves in pilot purgatory.

Done right, the organization learns and iterates in the relentless OV cycle of observing, accepting, and acting; everyone constantly discovers new information, tests hypotheses, and acts. This ensures actions have variety—and are unpredictable, accelerating your momentum and putting your competitors on roller skates.

The Joy of Discovery

Our basic emotions are negative—and numerous. Fear, disgust, anger, sadness, and surprise dominate our mindset. The small bets approach capitalizes on our one positive emotion: joy. It is an iterative testing process of learning that culminates in the joy of discovery.

You start with what you don't know. What you learn as you engage in the process of small bets leads to additional hypotheses that are then tested. The entire OV process can be thought of as one of discovery versus testing. For example, in-market tests for a new product, you're typically looking for something specific such as product acceptance, willingness to pay, or the relative value of product features. Discovery is being open to customer responses you didn't expect. The process of testing, engaging directly with the external environment on a problem or opportunity of significance, *puts you in a position to discover*. In the OV process, this is a critical input to the Observe phase. You don't have to go far to find someone with a story about how someone went to an industry event and discovered a great opportunity through a chance encounter. You've probably also heard stories from people who went to industry events and were bored to tears. Testing is predictable; discovery is not.

In the early days of e-commerce, my colleagues and I at UPS developed a shipping solution that allowed manufacturers to create shipments using the same system as their suppliers; everyone would know what is being shipped, when it was shipped, and when it arrived. We took the solution to a large auto manufacturer who tried it out and told us, "I wouldn't use it to ship on the same platform as my suppliers, but I would love to use this as a campus shipping solution. It would be of great value to the company if we could administer shipping across the campus to reduce out-of-contract purchases." We hadn't thought of that. In testing solution A, we discovered solution B, which UPS later rolled out under the brand name CampusShip. Only by actively engaging with the external environment—your partners, your customers, your broader stakeholder groups, can you put yourself in a position to discover.

The power of the small bets strategy is that it allows you to discover the right solution as opposed to confirming the right solution. How much time and money is wasted in businesses today debating a course of action that can never be discovered within the enterprise's four walls?

Rethink the Game. Redefine Risk

The genius of OV companies is that they are not trying to beat anyone at their game. They are rethinking the game entirely. This includes how they reorient their employees' understanding of risk to be more willing to engage in behaviors that propel the firm forward.

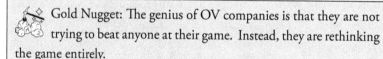

Gold Nugget: The genius of OV companies is that they are not trying to beat anyone at their game. Instead, they are rethinking the game entirely.

The key is to redefine risk as part of the process of discovery and future success. Then, change the culture to embrace risk.

Japanese companies, excellent at sustaining businesses over the long term, are now creating a *dejima* to allow risk-averse managers to experience trial and error. The word means "exit island," an autonomous Dutch trading post hidden from Japanese society during the Edo period.[3] As an incubator for new opportunities, the *dejima* is somewhat isolated in a beneficial way; it allows employees to experience what failure feels like and how it can lead to future success. It creates a safe zone for risk-taking. Company leaders can encourage managers to take on challenges without fear of failure and not punish them during annual performance reviews.

---

[3] J. Yanagisawa. January 28, 2020. "The 'Dejima' Strategy for Promoting Open Innovation in Companies: Creating an Investment Return Framework, Not a Cost Center," *NRI Journal.* www.nri.com/en/journal/2020/0128

Over time, the *dejima* changes the culture from many risk-averse isolated units into an organization with a risk-taking mentality.

The acid test for whether a company is embracing risk or paying it lip service is to see what happens when a risky project goes wrong. Kevin O'Meara is a supply chain vice president at Shaw Industries that inherited a very large project with some very large problems. By the time his team determined the project was sinking, they had already spent a lot of money and had committed even more. As is typical of OV leaders, Kevin did not cower, hide the evidence, or distribute blame. He said they were going to the CapEx committee and would tell them we made a mistake. "So Mea Culpa, we're wrong, but the right thing for the company is to stop the project and acknowledge we were wrong. Shaw calls these meetings 'after-action' reviews, and the goal is learning." O'Meara continued, "We went into the committee and, I've got to tell you, that was when I knew I had joined the right company and found a home. There wasn't any person in that meeting, including our CEO and CFO, who went down the path of whose fault, why did this happen? Insinuating that somebody's head has got to roll, which absolutely would have happened in other companies I've been." O'Meara's manager, Executive Vice President David Morgan then posed the quintessential OV question, "Okay, we paid the tuition, now what did we learn?" That's what happens when you can be vulnerable; you become a learning company. Said O'Meara, "It's what did we learn today, not what we know."[4]

 Gold Nugget: An OV leader responds to a failure by saying, "Okay, we paid the tuition; now what did we learn?"

Breaking the Bureaucracy

Haier's microenterprises is a recent successful example of reorienting a company around taking risks. Haier is a modular structure on steroids, not too different from the "pizza teams" at Amazon (e.g., individual teams

---

[4] Video interview with Kevin O'Meara, December 21, 2020.

shouldn't be larger than what two pizzas can feed). Haier CEO Zhang Ruimin, who has always been obsessed with breaking the bureaucracy, issued midlevel managers an ultimatum: either be fired or become independent entrepreneurs. It was "the hardest decision" the CEO had ever made, but it was meant to transform the company from a few monolithic businesses into some 4,000 microenterprises, or MEs, most comprising just 10 to 15 employees.[5]

Zhang turned his company into a hive with a mindset of "one for all and all for one." He gave the leaders of each ME the suite of decision-making powers regarding strategy, people, and distribution. He also introduced several internal platforms to facilitate transactions among MEs, likening the idea to an app store. It enabled coordination but did not direct it. It also gave MEs the freedom to adjust their own supply chains according to specialized knowledge and up-to-date information. They could then act rapidly to reduce disruption and recover more quickly than their competitors. During the pandemic, these MEs buoyed the business by responding to market changes more swiftly than competitors.

Allowing for employee entrepreneurship is how you till the ground for OV to bloom.

Separating from the Death Hug

Haier's microenterprises show what can happen when a company liberates all units to observe, accept, and act. They can innovate at speed because they are not subject to the drag of processes typical of a centrally structured hierarchy. Creating velocity demands being separate from the drag of archaic MBA-modeled decision-making processes.

Some firms, like Haier, decentralize their entire structure to speed up decision making and learning. Still, others create a separate innovation group or innovation environment. Top corporate innovation labs include GoogleX, Amazon Lab126, Coca-Cola's KOLab, and Lowe's Innovation Lab. Family-owned businesses may have a distinct advantage over public

---

[5] https://hbr.org/2018/11/the-end-of-bureaucracy

companies by the mere fact that executives can "act like founders," even if they are third or fourth-generation leaders. Founder-led companies don't always have pedigrees, but they have a philosophy about how a company should act and behave. This often translates into less bureaucracy, leading to less friction and increased speed.

The common factor for companies that succeed at being innovative is their commitment to "keeping a wall around innovation, so the mothership doesn't hug it to death." The "mothership" can hug new innovations to death by not distinguishing between efficiency and exploration. This can take the form of continuous progress reports, or "Committee Roulette," to get approval for every move forward, expecting a short-term financial return. Business planning for innovation is an act of futility. Once you start measuring innovation projects with ROIC or NPV, you're encouraging managers to invest in sure things. Real innovation is never a sure thing.

 Gold Nugget: Keep a wall around innovation, so the Mothership doesn't hug it to death.

Benchmark the Best

Who would you look to as a beacon of OV, an organization to aspire to? Consider the challenge ING CIO Peter Jacobs faced transforming a traditional financial services company with roots dating back to 1762 into an agile firm able to change continuously. Jacobs recognized the hypocrisy of claiming agility without addressing the existing organizational structure and governance. They stopped benchmarking against other banks and began learning from technology firms. ING adopted peer-to-peer hiring from Google, and an onboarding program inspired by Zappos.[6]

---

[6] P. Jacobs, B. Schlatmann, and D. Mahadevan. January 10, 2017. "ING's Agile Transformation," *The McKinsey Quarterly*.

Change Your Metrics

Innovations, by definition, are not predictable. Your metrics should focus on learning—speed of learning, quality of learning, and percent of pilots that turn into commercial offerings over a two-to-three-year period. The most important financial metric at this stage is gross margin. A sufficient group of customers must receive enough value from the innovation to pay you more than the cost of providing the value.

Your metrics should also reflect how customers drive the innovation that delivers more significant gross margins. Amazon has changed the metrics with its cell-based network. And it's all based on their core value of being customer-obsessed. The cell-based network creates an intense focus on a problem to solve directly related to a clear relationship with the external customer, not internal customers that shift your focus inward. This kind of innovation travels outside-in: from the outside customer into upper management. A corresponding good metric is the number of innovative projects being overseen by senior management. Companies like Texas Health Resources use executive sponsors that "own" the project to ensure it achieves its value and meets user expectations.[7]

Outside the Mothership

Established organizations may need to let new initiatives grow outside the mothership. For example, a Fortune 50 consumer goods company was buying small brands that weren't succeeding inside the big brand company. The company switched to incubating these smaller brands outside the company with their own teams and metrics to great success. When I was with the UPS Logistics and Distribution business, we didn't do so well with a similar scenario. We purchased some well-run health care logistics companies in Europe that went from stars to dogs in a matter of months. Did we get fooled? Did management stop executing?

---

[7] "The Role of the Executive Sponsor in Healthcare Technology Projects," www.healthleadersmedia.com/innovation/role-executive-sponsor-healthcare-technology-projects (accessed August 25, 2009).

No. UPS just applied its higher non-operations cost to the smaller company, and margins deteriorated.

This is another area where the Board of Directors plays a critical role. Someone on the board needs to take an active part in guiding the innovation business unit. This will help the CEO manage the inevitable trade-offs between the innovation businesses and the core business.

Other established organizations set up separate entities within the organization to avoid the death hug. Former SAP executive Gil Perez employed this strategy by creating a competency center to encourage free thinking. He created spaces where workshops could be created, staffed with coaches who could do design thinking with customers and internally. "Over time," he told me, "everybody got certified or was engaged in a design thinking session."[8]

Perhaps the best way to keep the mothership from smothering innovation is to make everyone an innovator. This is the ultimate goal. Former Alibaba Group executive Lee McCabe scoffed at the position of Chief Innovation Officer at many big companies. "Everyone should be a chief innovations officer. Innovation should be a part of the culture, with everyone encouraged to question and test everything. Even as every customer is humming in digital reaction, every employee should have a digital mind."[9]

 Gold Nugget: Everyone should be a Chief Innovation Officer.

The Alibaba executive is defining not only a tech-oriented culture. He is describing tech as the only way of life within an organization. Implicit in an OV organization is a competency to develop and improve its technological skills and capabilities. Especially since the half-life of a learned technical skill is estimated to be less than five years, meaning a

---

[8] G. Perez. September 19, 2018. "Chief Innovation Officer, Deutsche Bank, Former SVP Products & Innovation, SAP." Interview by Alan Amling.

[9] L. McCabe. September 25, 2018. "Operating Partner, AEA Investors LP, Former Vice President North America, Alibaba." Interview by Alan Amling.

skill learned today will be about half as valuable in less than five years.[10] According to the World Economic Forum, artificial intelligence and machine learning technologies will create the need for over 133 million new technology roles between 2019 and 2022.[11] Companies that understand the implications of the widening tech skills gap are investing heavily in this skill development. For example, Amazon launched its in-house Machine Learning University in 2016.[12]

Right Leaders with the Right Stuff

As I have stressed throughout this book, all mindset shifts within an organization hinge on leadership. OV organizations require the strongest kind of leaders. The question is how to find them.

A typical approach is to cultivate the most promising performers within an organization. However, the best players are not always the best leaders. What helps an individual succeed—talent, hard work, and discipline—does not always correlate to success in leadership. The best leaders or coaches are the ones that can bring the most out of each individual while orchestrating a 1+1=3 symbiotic relationship with everyone else in the organization.

Professional sports demonstrate this. Bill Belichick was not a household name as a player at Wesleyan University but became the winningest coach in NFL history. On the other hand, Wayne Gretsky (aka "The Great One") had a lackluster career as coach of the Phoenix Coyotes. So why did Belichick and others like Mike Ditka and Phil Jackson succeed

---

[10] "Skill, Re-Skill and Re-Skill Again. How to Keep up with the Future of Work," *World Economic Forum.* www.weforum.org/agenda/2017/07/skill-reskill-prepare-for-future-of-work/ (accessed July 31, 2017).

[11] M. Milano. March 12, 2019. "The Digital Skills Gap is Widening Fast. Here's How to Bridge it," *World Economic Forum.* www.weforum.org/agenda/2019/03/the-digital-skills-gap-is-widening-fast-heres-how-to-bridge-it/

[12] D. Gantenbein. 2020. "Amazon's Machine Learning University is Making its Online Courses Available to the Public," *Amazon Science.* www.amazon.science/latest-news/machine-learning-course-free-online-from-amazon-machine-learning-university

while star players didn't? Perhaps the single most significant factor is that they were understudies of the best NFL coaches of all time, Belichick under Bill Parcels and Ditka under Tom Landry. Jackson honed his skills over eleven seasons as an NBA assistant.

Of course, great players can become great leaders, but it's not guaranteed they will. Companies often make the mistake of assuming a high-performing employee also has the right stuff for leadership. As a result, they will push high performers into management regardless of their motivations or skillsets. A Gallup study found that companies fail to choose the right manager for the job 82 percent of the time. Why? The top two reasons are previous success in non-managerial roles and their tenure with the company.[13]

Conversely, successful OV companies seek leaders who engender trust and have exhibited the Disruptor Trifecta introduced in chapter 4; they possess good judgment, know the industry, and are tech-savvy. Consequently, they know how to establish goals and boundaries and what to do with their data. Access to technology is table stakes; how firms use the technology separates the good from the great. A golfer can have the best clubs and balls available, but it's the golfer's skill that will make the ball fly true. In addition, disruptive leaders must be ambidextrous, skilled at balancing growth and efficiency. Most managers are comfortable with efficiency; few can combine it with a mindset conducive to exploration and leaning into the unknown.

 Truth Bomb: Access to technology is table stakes; how firms use the technology separates the good from the great.

I return to Bill Belichick because he is also the most disruptive coach. He constantly confuses the opposing team and maximizes opportunities in the disrupted environment. Belichick's genius is not just his ability to devise efficient systems to handle a football game's complex and high-speed flow. He also knows how to manage players, most of whom are

[13] Inc. Gallup. April 08, 2015. *State of the American Manager.* www.gallup.com/services/182138/state-american-manager.aspx

not superstars. What they are is teachable, and what they learn is the "Belichick Way." They are led by a coach who leans into the unknown with every game. The genius of Belichick is less a matter of strategy than of team-building.

A great leader looks for the right people to lead. To get people to lean into risk and delight in discovery, a leader must first inspire them. You know when you've inspired them because they are doing things because they want to, not because they have to. They are doing the work that propels the firm forward, even when it's not part of their performance metrics, and nobody is looking over their shoulder.

Going back to the golf analogy, buying the best clubs won't necessarily improve a golfer's game. The real battle is for the hearts and minds of people swinging the clubs. Running an OV organization is more than surviving digital disruption and implementing a digital strategy with digital people.

The legendary UCLA coach John Wooden built a wildly successful basketball program based on a philosophy of life he called the Pyramid of Success. The cornerstones are industriousness and enthusiasm, as characterized by people who are passionate, positive, and completely present to every person and task in front of them.[14] Wooden was all about the fundamentals. My Uncle sent me to a John Wooden basketball camp when I was in high school. I had grand visions of playing games all day and sinking a few shots in front of the Wizard of Westwood. Much to my dismay, we did drills for three days straight before we ever played a game. He knew if you weren't willing to put in the time off the court, you wouldn't be worth your time on the court. The Pyramid of Success was not just about success in basketball; it was about success in life. Industriousness and enthusiasm need to be cornerstones of your OV organizations.

 Truth Bomb: Industriousness and enthusiasm are the cornerstones of success.

---

[14] J. Wooden, J. Tobin, and B. Walton. 1988. *They Call Me Coach*. Contemporary Books Chicago.

To find potential OV leaders from within the organization, put people on your skunkworks, pilots, and other experiments. Challenge them. Put them in uncomfortable situations. Adversity will reveal their character, one way or another. Then, keep forcing those leaders who show an aptitude to move with OV to flex their OV muscles. Over time, and with enough leaders, you will have engrained OV into the fabric of your company.

Another trait of an OV leader is digital fluency. While you can admire people who become digitally savvy, be careful not to put them in positions that require digital fluency. At top positions, you need digital natives who have internalized technology and for whom it's second nature. Compare it with the difference between a student studying four years of Spanish—even studies abroad and is immersed in the language—and a native speaker from Costa Rica. They don't have to think about the language; it's part of who they are. Therefore, companies must develop OV leaders who are digital natives.

OV organizations must also create an environment where innovative ideas emerge. Karin Hut and David Dye from the University of Colorado found five reasons people don't speak up to contribute solutions, suggest innovations, or advocate for customers.[15]

1. People don't think leadership wants their ideas.
2. No one asks.
3. They lack the confidence to share (this is a learned behavior!).
4. They lack the skills to share effectively.
5. People don't think anything will happen, so they don't bother.

As discussed earlier, every idea left unsaid is a potential value the organization and the individual will never access. OV organizations get their people to tell them what they're thinking. And encourage them to "say

---

[15] K. Hurt and D. David. n.d. "5 Reasons Your Employees are Holding Back on Sharing Ideas," *Fast Company*. www.fastcompany.com/90526638/the-main-reasons-employees-dont-speak-their-mind-at-work

more." As the Japanese proverb goes, "The frog in the well knows nothing of the mighty ocean."[16]

Finally, OV organizations embrace diversity—not only of opinions but of experiences. Several years ago, I told a good friend that our son had told us he was gay. "We already knew it," I said, "and we were relieved he was comfortable enough to tell us. I want to understand how he feels so I can help him navigate his God-given path." At this, my friend laughed. "You have no more of a chance of understanding what it's like to be gay as you do to be black." Upon reflection, I realized she was right. It's lived experience that brings a diversity of thought. And it's the same with an organization. For true diversity within an organization, you need people who have lived different experiences. Just as biodiversity stabilizes an ecosystem, people of diverse backgrounds within an organization can help it thrive.

 Truth Bomb: It's lived experience that brings true diversity of thought.

In the end, the secret sauce of any OV organization is the people. Again, it's not about the golf clubs; the real battle is for the hearts and minds of the people swinging the clubs. Jim Casey did this early on with UPS. His clearly defined vision encouraged manager owners to be receptive to each other and their customers. It created an environment conducive to discovery.

Without the hearts and minds of your people, you'll spin your wheels. You'll go through the motions of being OV without going anywhere. You'll talk but won't do. At the end of the day, it doesn't matter if you have the technology or a great idea unless you first have the mindset, a compelling vision, a direction with boundaries, and, most of all, the people who are permitted to speak up and even fail.

---

[16] S. Parrish. June 12, 2017. "Thought Experiment: How Einstein Solved Difficult Problems," *Farnam Street, Farnam Street.* https://fs.blog/2017/06/thought-experiment/

What?

OV cannot survive in a heirarchial organization built for control.

So What?

Great intentions become innovation theater and broken promises to employees and customers in a friction-packed organization.

Now What?

Become an OV company. Get off your heels and go on offense. Remove friction in the organization, reduce the team size to promote agility and accountability, embrace diversity, align your metrics, and discover your future with small bets. Hire, develop, and promote leaders demonstrating an OV mindset.

CHAPTER 8

You Can't Hug Data

Acting Through Supply Chain

Leaders win through logistics. Vision, sure. Strategy, yes. But when you go to war, you need to have both toilet paper and bullets at the right place at the right time. In other words, you must win through superior logistics.

—Tom Peters

Few business transformations in recent years were more unforeseen than that of Fujifilm. Many still think of Fujifilm as the green-and-white miniature boxes of 35 mm film that sit next to Kodak's gold boxes at the local pharmacy. But Fujifilm is no Kodak. Fujifilm took an alternative journey than that of Kodak's descent into oblivion. As the core photographic film market gave way to digital photography, Fujifilm refused to "stick to its core," the mantra of most legacy executives during times of societal and economic upheaval. As the film business shrank, Fujifilm started or grew other businesses, including medical systems, pharmaceuticals, regenerative medicine, life sciences, cosmetics, flat panel display (FPD) materials, industrial products, electronic materials, recording media, and graphic systems.

The outlier seemed to be cosmetics. Of all the industries to tap, what drove Fujifilm to enter the cosmetics industry? It seems random, but it's an excellent example of John Boyd's famous snowmobile analogy.[1] In his presentations, Boyd would sometimes ask his audience to go on an imagi-

---

[1] J. Boyd. 1987. *Destruction and Creation*. U.S. Army Comand and General Staff College.

native journey: to imagine riding in an outboard motorboat pulling water skiers, or riding a bike on a spring day, or watching your son or daughter play with toy tractors or tanks with rubber caterpillar treads at a store. Then Boyd would walk his audience through the mental process of separating key elements from each image: skis, outboard motor, handlebars, and rubber treads. He then asked, "What emerges when you pull these elements together?"

His answer? The snowmobile.[2] This was precisely Fujifilm's strategy.

 Gold Nugget: Build snowmobiles; take stock of your existing assets and capabilities to create new value for your customers.

Color photographic film is about the same thickness as human hair. To manufacture film that retains moisture and maintains its shape requires collagen. Consequently, Fujifilm, whose core competencies included chemical engineering, understood how to manufacture and control various types of collagen. This capability was also required in the manufacturing of skincare products. As a result, Fujifilm's leadership took stock of the resources at its disposal and built, essentially, "snowmobiles," new products with existing "components" or competencies that made life better for consumers.

The 2020 pandemic forced many businesses to divert existing capabilities to manufacture products to battle COVID-19: Gap, Zara, and Brooks Brothers converted their factories to make masks, gowns, and scrubs. The Ford Motor Company partnered with 3M to produce medical equipment on its auto assembly lines. Nike converted portions of its factories to make face shields and air-purifying respirators. In partnership with Dow, SC Johnson converted a manufacturing facility in Wisconsin to produce 75,000 bottles of hand sanitizer per month. Bacardi shifted operations in eight distilleries to make the ethanol needed to manufacture hand sanitizer. Fiat Chrysler worked with Ferrari and its parent company Exor to manufacture ventilator parts in a plant in Italy.

---

[2] Boyd, *Destruction and Creation.*

The ability to adapt in the midst of a pandemic is a supply chain competency—and evidence of organizational velocity (OV). The pandemic exposed poor supply chains and rewarded great ones. Consumer priorities quickly switched from valuing price, quality, and features to just purchasing a product, any product. Few people passed on off-brand toilet paper in April 2020 so that they could "squeeze the Charmin."

Throughout the book, I've defined OV as the mindset and behavior of observing, accepting (or not), and acting (or not) on information from the external environment with speed and agility. The role of acting is, primarily, a supply chain exercise. It addresses the question, "How are we going to execute?"

Whether it's goods or services, execution requires accessing resources within the organization or acquiring resources from another organization through purchase or partnership, then turning those resources into products that make the life of the target consumer better. This is, in its most simple form, supply chain. Speed and agility in the Fourth Industrial Revolution must be applied not only to new product development but to the supply chain itself. In many ways, the two—product development and supply chain—have merged into one. Much like retailers are becoming logistics companies, technology giants are becoming financial services companies. Apple expanded into payments with Apple Card. PayPal now offers business loans and recently launched its own cryptocurrency service, allowing people to buy, hold, and sell digital currency on its site and applications.[3]

When Disney became a streaming company, it was a supply chain decision. When Netflix moved from streaming only Hollywood's movies to also producing original entertainment, it was also a supply chain decision. When DuPont's expertise with nitrocellulose in explosives was applied to cellulose-based plastics and fibers products, it was, pure and simple, a rethinking of the supply chain.

An OV leader expects and plans for disruptions to the supply chain. This demands that the leader constantly cast a wide net of observation of the external environment, quickly and correctly assess the impact of

---

[3] C. Alcorn. 2020. "Bitcoin Surges After Paypal Jumps into the Cryptocurrency Business," In *Markets Now* (CNN Business). www.cnn.com/2020/10/21/investing/paypal-bitcoin-cryptocurrencies/index.html

changes on the business and act with speed and agility. The ability to reimagine your business based on changes in the external environment is a fundamental tenant of OV.

Supply Chain Fundamentals

No business, small or large, will thrive if it can't keep its promises. Supply chain is how the brand promise is delivered. Consequently, every company has a supply chain. Even a small software company in the tech corridor of your city has a supply chain. Its raw material is intellectual capital. Where will this tech firm source its talent? What criteria does it use to attract, assess, and retain talent? The software company has the same supply chain tensions as the manufacturing facility just down the road: how does its leadership allocate resources between developing the next version of the current product or design completely new products? It is easy to conceptualize a supply chain for a manufactured good, but these networks also exist for services and products that are digitally delivered.

At its essence, a supply chain consists of an organization's people, activities, information, and resources needed to move a product or service from the origins of supply all the way to the point of final consumption. Increasingly, this system extends to re-entering material that was not consumed back into the supply chain for reuse or recycling. Put more crisply, a supply chain transforms raw materials and ideas into products and services that improve the lives of consumers. Note the last phrase of the previous sentence—"that improves the lives of consumers."

There is an organization's supply chain, and then there is its *supply chain management*, the ability to move with speed and agility—and to "act," as I mentioned earlier. I serve as a Distinguished Fellow at the University of Tennessee, where we define *supply chain management* as "the systematic coordination of traditional business functions within a particular organization and across organizations within the supply chain for the purposes of improving the long-term performance of the individual enterprises and the system as a whole."[4] This comprehensive definition recognizes that supply

---

[4] J.T. Mentzer, W. DeWitt, J.S. Keebler, S. Min, N.W. Nix, C.D. Smith, and Z.G. Zacharia. 2001. "Defining Supply Chain Management," *Journal of Business logistics* 22, no. 2.

chains exist within a broader external business environment, consisting of geopolitical forces, government regulations, industry and competitive factors, and the changing nature of markets and demand.

While the digital economy has been remaking industries for decades, the supply chain industry had been relatively untouched, save the incremental innovations that reduced time and cost while increasing capabilities and quality. The historical reality of the supply chain was that assets rule: the Silk Road could be traveled only with camels, and a company could navigate the global supply chain primarily with hard assets.

However, the nexus of persistent advantage is changing.

The shift is from the "those who own the assets" rule to the "those who own the customer" rule. Increasingly, asset owners in the supply chain are not calling the shots; they are on the receiving end of the shots. And the customer rules. Simply because the Internet has given them access to the greatest source of power since the dawn of time—information. No company survives long term by shorting their customer. Especially today, because alternatives are a click away.

Nordstrom, for example, has given its customers access to the power of information. It has created accessible, accurate supply chain data that allows employees to see what inventory the company has throughout the company. More critical, salespeople can then control the movement of any item in inventory to the benefit of their customers. The transparent supply chain empowers salespeople to deliver excellent customer service. And over time, that same supply chain transparency has given online customers access to Nordstrom's entire inventory, whether an item is on a rack at a store or in a warehouse waiting for shipment.

Transparency empowers customers to give supply chain commands. While Nordstrom is no Amazon, Nordstrom's supply chain transparency keeps the company relevant and allows it to focus on responding to competitor initiatives and conducting new digital business experiments. Nordstrom has created a capability that the company can reuse even as the business itself becomes more complex.

A Veruca Salt World

One of the most memorable characters from the movie *Charlie and the Chocolate Factory* is Veruca Salt, the immature, over-indulged young girl who managed to secure one of the GoldenTickets. Unfortunately, no price for her demands was too ridiculous; her affluent parents wouldn't say no. So when the spoiled brat didn't immediately get what she wanted, she screamed and stomped until she succeeded. Veruca Salt is a caricature of the quintessential customer of the Fourth Industrial Revolution. We all are Veruca Salt. We want exactly what we want, when and where we want it— and at the lowest possible cost. It doesn't matter if you're in manufacturing, insurance, health care, or retail; your customer is Veruca Salt.

 Truth Bomb: We all are Veruca Salt. We want exactly what we want, when and where we want it—and at the lowest possible cost.

The e-commerce kettle has been brewing since the mid-1990s, but it boiled over during the pandemic. McKinsey estimated e-commerce growth accelerated by ten years in the first three months of 2020.[5] Whether you're selling cars, paintings, or hot air fryers, everything is moving online where selection is unlimited. A simple search for "light bulbs" on Amazon.com will return more than 10,000 results. Are you looking for a specific whiskey? Binny's Beverage Depot has over 1,200 brands for your selection pleasure. A typical Walmart Supercenter carries about 120,000 items, but you can find over 35 million on Walmart.com.[6]

Of course, you can't drive, eat, or hug data. We are living in a material world (nod to Madonna), and for most products, digital dreams must be transformed into physical realities. Therein lies the rub. How do you satisfy Veruca's demands for speed, selection, and quality?

Veruca wants what she wants. She may not walk into a Target store expecting to buy an Italian gas cooktop, but she can find it at Target.com and have it delivered for free. If you don't have it available, your competition is only a click away.

---

[5] Mckinsey & Company. July 28, 2020. "The Quickening," Survey, *McKinsey Quarterly*. www.mckinsey.com/business-functions/strategy-and-corporate-finance/our-insights/five-fifty-the-quickening

[6] T. Walk-Morris. July 30, 2020. "Walmart's Marketplace Doubles in a Year: Report," *Retail Dive*. www.retaildive.com/news/walmarts-marketplace-doubles-in-a-year-report/582599/

Veruca wants it now. A 2020 survey of retailers indicated that 71 percent planned to offer next-day or same-day delivery by 2022.[7] Amazon has led the way, investing over $60 billion in 1-Day Prime delivery. Their big-box competitors like Walmart, Target, Best Buy, and Petsmart are upping the game by turning their massive footprint of retail stores into fulfillment centers. This enables same-day shipping powered by a combination of store employees, gig-workers, and contractors coordinated through powerful AI-enabled routing software.

Veruca wants it at the lowest possible cost. Moving physical goods across a network versus moving packets of information are night and day different. Understand, however, that it's your problem, not Veruca's. And solving for speed, selection, and cost is only half the battle. It must be done despite labor constraints, ESG (Environmental, Social, and Governance) considerations, geopolitical unrest, natural disasters, and constant cybersecurity threats. In this environment, OV is not an option; it's a requirement.

Companies will need to become MMA fighters, able to sense and respond, pivot instinctively. The elements of OV will be your roadmap:

Observe

- Use technology to cast a wide net of observation.
- Become comfortable being uncomfortable; explore emerging technologies and business models.

Accept

- Use technology to separate the signal from the noise.
- Block the "blockers."
- Hire/promote diversity of thought to reduce blind spots.
- Create boundaries allowing decision making to be pushed to the edge, closest to the customer.
- Use your Board as an asset, not a gatekeeper.

---

[7] *Perspectives on Retail and Consumer Goods*, McKinsey & Company (August, 2020).

Act

- Foster rapid learning using a small bets strategy and autonomous teams.
- Align hiring, promotion, and compensation to encourage OV actions.
- Build snowmobiles; take stock of your existing assets and capabilities to create new value.
- Create a compelling narrative that unites a distributed workforce around a common mission.
- Eliminate organizational friction—expand information access, raise spending authority, and reduce time-sucking committees and meetings.
- Build your capabilities, creating new options you can leverage in times of threat or opportunity.
- Celebrate OV actions within your company.

OV is happening today in the supply chain. Retailers are building snowmobiles when they convert a physical store to a fulfillment operation. Inventory is getting pushed closer to consumers. Carriers are balancing ESG concerns and costs by adding electric vehicles to their fleet. Perhaps the most significant change is how the supply chain is viewed within the organization from a mindset perspective. Is it a cost center or a strategic asset? If your Chief Supply Chain officer or equivalent title is not reporting directly to your CEO or, in some cases, COO, you have work to do. Veruca Salt is waiting.

Merging Worlds

Digital supply chains start with the consumer and are built back to the source, not the other way around. On the other hand, traditional manufacturing is designed around mega-factories in low-cost countries, making millions of the same widget. Demand forecasting, upon which the conventional supply chain was built, imperfectly manages bulk movements from supply centers to demand centers, where goods are stored and shipped to retailers or consumers as needed. While supply chains can absorb shock(s) and quickly respond to interruptions to a certain extent, the magnitude of disruptions in 2020 eclipsed their capacity to adapt. Increasingly, the centralized manufacturing model in low-cost countries supported by lengthy supply chains will be challenged by on-demand consumers who increasingly want customized goods and delivery as close to now as possible.

As Veruca Salt drives on-demand production, the historically separate elements of manufacturing and supply chain necessarily merge. On-demand requires greater coordination between manufacturing and supply chain, including regional/local product availability. This can quickly become an inventory nightmare unless Industry 4.0 technologies are used. One such technology is blockchain, a kind of digital diary that is virtually impossible to forge. An easy way to think of the components of a blockchain is to use the analogy of train tracks. The railroad ties equate to a block of data, the track is the chain connecting one block to another, and the train is the application that operates on top of the track. Multiple parties need to agree on where to place each railroad tie. Theoretically, one party could move the railroad tie, but not without removing the track and with the other parties agreeing where to move the railroad tie. This is why blockchain is said to be immutable.

> Gold Nugget: As Veruca Salt drives on-demand production, the historically separate elements of manufacturing and supply chain necessarily merge.

Revisiting the blockchain story from chapter three, Walmart Canada deployed the technology to pay freight bills from trucking companies. As one of the largest truckload shippers in the country, Walmart Canada partners with approximately 60 for-hire carriers to move millions of pounds of freight annually. Each invoice (or freight load) generated 200 data elements. This profusion of data created an abundance of invoicing issues. In fact, disputes affected 70 percent of invoices, resulting in long delays in processing payments to the carriers. In addition, Walmart Canada personnel spent a considerable amount of non-valued added time determining how to assign charges to a specific load. Partnering with DLT Labs, Walmart Canada deployed a customized blockchain solution

(DL Freight) for its freight invoice and payments system.[8] The solution provided a single ledger with consistent data.

While blockchain is a disruptive digital technology, Walmart Canada's application to its invoicing crisis was, at least in the narrow definition of innovation, more of a sustaining innovation.[9] When applied to track and trace, provenance, payment processing, managing IoT networks, medical record sharing, smart contracts, and digital content distribution, blockchain's benefits tend to be incremental. It's a problem Clayton Christensen identified in *The Innovator's Dilemma*: "If, as most successful companies try to do, a company stretches or forces a disruptive technology to fit the needs of current, mainstream customers ... it is almost sure to fail." Blockchain is no silver bullet, though that doesn't mean the technology shouldn't be applied to improve existing processes. But a technology, such as blockchain, is truly disruptive when it does more than sustain innovation.

Another digital technology, Additive Manufacturing (AM), mentioned in previous chapters, is increasingly enabling distributed manufacturing. Customized goods can be produced in lower quantities, more often, and closer to the point of consumption. This eliminates portions of the storage and shipping process (old-school supply chain elements). It unleashes agility and flexibility as local manufacturers closer to the customer tailor products to smaller groups of consumers or even individuals.

A simple example is Adidas's FutureCraft line of shoes.[10] Its midsole is 3D Printed and can be customized to an individual's weight, gait, and usage. Imagine the data that Adidas is collecting with its brand. And how it's customizing its supply chain to its Veruca Salt consumer mindset. This type of technology is like the proverbial pond with one lily pad that doubles every day. As I explained in chapter 2, the growth on such a

---

[8] N. Tabak. September 08, 2020. "How Walmart Used Blockchain to End Freight Payment Woes in Canada," *FreightWaves*. www.freightwaves.com/news/how-walmart-solved-canada-carrier-payment-woes-with-blockchain

[9] C.M. Christensen. 2013. *The Innovator's Dilemma: When New Technologies Cause Great Firms to Fail*, 226. Harvard Business Review Press.

[10] "Adidas Futurecraft," *Adidas US*. www.adidas.com/us/futurecraft (accessed June 28, 2021).

small base goes unnoticed for a long time until lily pads cover 25 percent of the pond, the next day 50 percent, and by the next day, it's covered completely. Competing shoe companies may look at solutions like FutureCraft and scoff. They may be right. There are always a hundred different reasons a lily pad innovation dies. When they're not right, it could be devastating to their business. The lily pad proliferation swallows them. That they "never saw it coming" was a choice, not a circumstance. OV companies observe the few lily pads on the pond and ensure they are ready to pivot by making small bets in areas like AM so they can move and adapt quickly.

OV companies take stock of both the known and the unknown. In this situation, what is known is that consumer expectations seldom go in reverse. As I have noted, customers want what they want. Go to any website or store selling athletic shoes, and you'll see hundreds of styles in various sizes and colors. If customers could get a shoe made specifically for their body and style at a comparable price to other choices, wouldn't they take it? Of course they would; this is known. What is unknown is whether the mass customization of shoes can be accomplished at a price point consumers will accept. OV companies don't wait for the answer; they discover it by making small bets in the space to speed learning and build new supply chain capabilities. Adidas bet that customers will demand customized shoes and are building optionality with their FutureCraft venture.

While UPS is not in the shoe business, AM could have an equally disruptive impact on UPS. UPS's core business is essentially to store and ship products, two activities that would be exponentially reduced if this technology for mass customization takes hold. Why? If AM could be done cost-effectively for a single, customized shoe, then the ripple effect would flow through the supply chain. Manufacturing would become decentralized, and products could be produced closer to the point of consumption. In addition, there would be little need for massive warehouses to store goods waiting to be purchased because demand (exactly what the customer wants) would be known in advance.

UPS, or any other firm, cannot change trends on its own. It is what it is. An OV company would observe the changes in manufacturing, accept that this could impact them ... or not, and act accordingly ... or not. Every company faces these moments from time to time. UPS decided to act on this potentially disruptive innovation. It was a difficult path. Spending resources exploring the unknown competes with spending resources on the known. In this case, AM represented a potential threat that may or may not materialize.

I led the exploration of AM at UPS. In 2014, UPS invested in a startup called Fast Radius, an AM initiative in the logistics space. Fast Radius' first Additive Micro-Factory (AMF) was launched on the UPS Supply Chain Campus in Louisville in May 2015. Fast Radius could receive an order in the afternoon, manufacture it, and then have it delivered anywhere in the United States by the next morning.

The original vision for Fast Radius was to build micro-factories in every global UPS Logistics Park, where small volume and/or customized products could be made and then delivered. UPS would then be part of this emerging supply chain, not a victim of it. What we learned was that the technology was not yet ready for prime time. Like so many disruptive technologies, the initial cost was too high, quality too low, and production speed and material availability left much to be desired. This is the challenge of the "S-curve."

When companies pursue the "act" phase of OV, they will often experience the all-too-common S-curve. Essentially, new products go through inflection points. In the early days, expenses are high and sales are low as companies build their market share. The product will bend toward profitability if things go well until eventually plateauing and declining, creating the entire "S." The challenge is, when you're in the early days of the trough, you don't know how long that will last. If you've ever been there, you know it's a lonely place. The naysayers have the upper hand, and the status quo forces will try to divert resources back to the "known." While UPS still has an investment in Fast Radius, the S-curve trough and another unknown, the COVID-19 pandemic, diverted attention and resources back to the core business in 2020. The existential threat of AM remains, but the desire to prepare for it has waned.

OV companies realize that acting is never the end of the process. Acting allows the company to capture both financial and knowledge capital. The new knowledge capital renews the observe-accept-act process. UPS, like all companies, had a choice to make when mired in the trough of the "S" curve. Overcome the organizational friction that throws sand in the OV gears or create the next iteration of learning.

In UPS's case, the opportunity to invest more into Fast Radius took a turn in June 2021 when Fast Radius announced a $1.4B SPAC (Special Purpose Acquisition Company) deal that will make them a public company in the fourth quarter of 2021. As a result, the financial return on UPS's investment in Fast Radius will pay out in spades, but the strategic value drops. Fast Radius no longer needs UPS's deep pockets to reach scale. The lesson here is that UPS observed and accepted the potential opportunity and threat of AM but failed to treat it with the appropriate sense of urgency and resources. This is more common than not. Consider that Barnes and Noble sold books online, Blockbuster offered movies by mail, and Kodak invented digital photography. The time to double-down on investment is before success is obvious, as Honeywell did when facing competition from Nest Labs' smart-home thermostat.

 Truth Bomb: The time to double-down on investment is before success is obvious.

Forms of Friction

Only a full-on commitment to OV can enable companies to rethink their supply chains. What prevents OV is not the technology or a company's ability to acquire it. The issue is always friction, and it comes in a variety of forms, such as the C-Suite protectionist mindset and the errant thinking that it can defend the castle; its current competitive advantage and customer set.

This friction keeps organizations from "acting," the very behavior that creates change.

GM, Ford, and other incumbent automakers are attempting to enter the electric vehicle market out of necessity but also face the issues of an architecturally different product. The years of experience developing internal combustion engines may inhibit their ability to succeed. This is where OV comes to life. From the managers put on the project to the organizational structure and measurement systems, every decision carries with it this question: will you create friction or remove it?

Slade Gardner is a leading expert in advanced materials, manufacturing, and processes for mission-critical prototypes and replacement parts. Previously a Fellow at Lockheed Martin Space Systems, he developed and implemented next-generation solutions for complex molded hardware in the aerospace and aeronautical industries. In an interview, he told me that of the eighty customers that Big Metal Additive serves, only one is looking at how additive can change manufacturing; the others are simply using the technology to support their existing supply chains. In short, they are attempting to use the technology within the constraints of their existing manufacturing paradigms. Good is the enemy of great.[11] While improving efficiency may solve short-term problems, it doesn't create new business models, which is the promise of AM.

Slade says that one of the friction points in adopting AM is that it encompasses every science discipline. It requires systems thinking, and no one or no silo can be left out of the process. He said that everyone must be an "A" player because the mechanics, the dimensional control, the thermodynamics—every aspect of the manufacturing process must be rethought.

"Wherever you find friction in adopting AM," he says, "you find a 'B' player."[12]

 Truth Bomb: Wherever you find friction in an organization, you find a "B" player.

Executives don't need to know how to code in Python to be fluent in technology or be active participants in testing new concepts to support innovation. Likewise, they don't need to be scheduling shipments to drive the supply chain. However, they need to set the goals and boundaries under which all the supply chain decisions can be made. They need to focus on inputs and outputs, not the technical "sausage-making" between those two points. Doing so only adds friction to the supply, not remove it. And in a Veruca Salt world, friction in the supply chain is death. See Table 8.1 for seven questions to reduce your corporate friction.

---

[11] J. Collins. 2016. *Good to Great: Why Some Companies Make the Leap and Others Don't*. HarperCollins.

[12] S. Gardner. September 09, 2020. "President and Founder at Big Metal Additive." Interview by Alan Amling.

Table 8.1 *Seven questions to reduce corporate friction*

Seven questions to reduce corporate friction	
1	Will you fully fund the project or meter out funding through a series of incremental stage gates?
2	Will you dedicate some of your best and brightest to discover new growth or make innovation a distraction to an already overloaded group?
3	Will you allow many small bets to create rapid, truth-based learnings?
4	Will you embrace outcomes, good or bad, as learnings to propel the next step or bury them?
5	Will you accept certain short-term losses for uncertain long-term returns?
6	Will you unburden new businesses with the overhead load of existing business?
7	Will you discourage the "blockers" concerned with protecting what they have?

To stay ahead of disruption requires a relentless focus on making lives (the customers', not the executives') better. Technology isn't disruptive because it's new; it's disruptive when it helps people do what they already needed to do, helping them solve for insufficient wealth, access, skill, or time.[13] To be an OV leader means to embrace the journey, not the hype. A company touting pilot projects that never turn into products, or whipsawing their investments in innovation, is a tell-tale sign that the company is not operating with OV.

At Cainiao Smart Logistics annual industry summit in Hangzhou in 2020, Daniel Zhang, Alibaba Group CEO and chairman of Cainiao Smart Logistics Network said, "Only through building the digital infrastructure for logistics can we truly enable and push the industry forward." As Alibaba's logistics platform operator, Cainiao Network owns few traditional logistics assets, like those of UPS and FedEx. Yet Cainiao processes the

---

[13] M.W. Johnson, C.M. Christensen, and H. Kagermann. 2008. "Reinventing Your Business Model," *Harvard Business Review* 86, no. 12.

majority of parcels shipped in China every day through their open platform coordinating 3,000 logistics partners and 3 million couriers.[14]

Cainiao aims to connect 100 million smart devices to its IoT technologies in three years, including its connected devices, warehouse and delivery robots, and algorithm-backed management systems. Logistics can no longer be an afterthought for any company but an integral part of digital infrastructure in today's world.

Whether you're a family-owned business or a publicly traded corporation, whether you're in services, retail, manufacturing, or logistics, disruption to your supply chain is coming to a theater near you. Only those who implement the principles of OV will be able to thrive in what's to come.

What?

The third component of OV, acting, converts ideas into action. The supply chain brings digital dreams to life.

So What?

Fast decision making will hit an execution brick wall if there is friction in the supply chain. Time is collapsing on the physical world. Demanding consumers will abandon the slow and static for the fast and nimble.

Now What?

The reality of a "right now" world is not a question of "if"; it's a question of when. So prepare your organization to observe, accept, AND act. Building advanced manufacturing and logistics capabilities, exploring new business models, and building your tech-savvy bench must be done now. The lily pads will soon be covering the pond.

---

[14] C. Campbell. November 23, 2020. "Chinese Company Cainiao Could Revolutionize Global Logistics," *Time.* https://time.com/5914173/cainiao-logisitics-alibaba-china-trade/

CHAPTER 9

How Shall You Then Live?

The problem in my life and other people's lives is not the absence of knowing what to do, but the absence of doing it.
—Peter Drucker

There are times to persist. There are times to start over. And the decision is rarely uncomplicated.

Rick Smith worked for a global executive search and leadership consulting practice. As an executive in the firm, Rick had daily conversations with global CEOs and board of directors about the qualities and experiences they sought in leaders. He had an idea: "We should create cohorts of the top leaders in different functional areas and create exclusive private groups. No video. No recordings. Just transparent communities where executives can be free to talk among their peers. And then we'll occasionally invite high profile guests to raise new or provocative issues."

When Rick pitched the idea to the executive team, heads nodded.

"Why don't you carve out some time and work on this," the CEO said, "and develop the concept a bit more."

He did. As the idea matured, the executives ostensibly viewed his efforts like a hobby: "Very interesting. We see the possibilities. Let's take another look at it." This is classic: kick the proverbial can down the road. No decisions. No resources other than Rick's time. Time rolled on. Increasingly, he spent more of his waking hours on the idea, and his conviction grew. Until that fateful day.

"We love what you've done with this project," his boss said. "It's clear, though, that your passion is no longer in our primary work that drives our revenue. We're going to let you go."

He wasn't wrong to fire Rick, but the termination put Rick into a tailspin.

Unemployed, he still believed in the concept. But he felt he had too little liquidity to fund a startup. Shortly after leaving the firm, Rick thought: "Maybe I'll start with marketing. And see if I can create a coalition of top marketing executives." He reached out to the Chief Marketing Officer (CMO) of Kodak, someone he had met several years back. Rick wasn't even sure the executive would remember him. He did. Rick pitched him on the vision for an exclusive, invitation-only group for elite marketing executives.

"This is fantastic," the CMO said. "I spend so much on conferences, but I don't really get to ask the questions that I want to ask from the people that have been through the battle—who understand exactly what I'm going through.

"You need to sign me up! How much is this?"

"It's $50,000 a year, an annual subscription."

He said it without stuttering. Truth be told, though, Rick hadn't even given pricing a thought. He wanted to make the service exclusive, and $50,000 was the number that came to mind.

"Hey, that's great! No problem," the CMO said. "Send the invoice to my assistant. We're good to go."

The call ended. And one of Rick's next thoughts was, "How do I create an invoice? I have no logo. I have nothing." He found a template online, made up a logo, and sent the invoice. Payment arrived almost immediately, though he didn't spend the $50,000. His next move was to reach out to another CMO who knew the one from Kodak: "We're only going to invite the top 50 companies in the country, so if you want to be part of this group, that's great, but we don't invite competitors. So, if two companies are competitors in the top 50, only one gets in."

It was called "The Marketing 50." He did the same for CFOs, CEOs, and even leaders in the supply chain and called it "World 50." Several years later, he sold it for a desirable price.[1]

The global recruiting firm gave Rick a gift for which he will be forever grateful: termination. Sometimes, it is exactly what we need to push us out of the corporate nest. Without being fired, though, it is almost

---

[1] R. Smith. n.d. "Founder: CNEXT, Fast Radius, World 50, G100 NGL, Bionic." Interview by Alan Amling, Multiple Interviews 2018–2019.

impossible to recognize when it is time to leave. Whether you're a CEO or middle manager, there's no guarantee that you'll be able to instill in the culture an organizational velocity (OV) mindset. There's a lot to be said for sticking it out. Your first decision, however, is not about how to change the organization. The first decision is about you. Only you control yourself. You cannot affect anything or influence anyone until you first change yourself. While this may seem patently obvious, I want to emphasize again: it is impossible to lead, wherever you are in the organization, without the right mindset, as I argued in chapter 2. You can't externalize the problem, complaining that "they just don't get it" if you have not bought into the values of OV.

 Truth Bomb: You cannot affect anything or influence anyone until you first change yourself.

I've discussed at length the superficial change in corporations that cannot resist the pullback to the status quo. OV is not sustainable unless the leader has done the hard work of ensuring the firm's people, structure, processes, and rewards are aligned. The story of my friend Rick illustrates a more profound truth for leaders. You need to look in the mirror, make sure you've checked your biases at the door, and have the mindset and capability to change. You have to believe in the principles of OV at your core. If you don't, you won't be able to sustain the work for a lifetime; you'll continue to make superficial moves, talk endlessly about the latest strategy fad, and "failing fast" and "think outside the box" and all the clichés of the modern organization.

It's like quitting a habit. You're not going to stop overeating because someone else wants you to. The motivation must come from within.

The Disparity Between Acting and Doing

A friend who is a committed Catholic often comments about how the mystery of the liturgy surprises him. The rituals of taking the sacrament and going to confession give him new insights into his life. Recently, after another round of confession in which he repented for the same sin, the priest asked, "Okay, well, are you going to do it again?"

My friend said he thought for a moment before he responded. "No," he said, "I'm not going to do it again. Wait, well, yes, I probably will do it again."

"You're wasting my time," the priest said and asked my friend to leave. That was a gut check for my friend who went on to transform his life.

Lip service is cheap. It doesn't demand sacrifice. If an organization, like the leadership consulting practice that Rick left, is unwilling to make sacrifices to survive, then talk of innovation is simply lip service.

Years ago, two Stanford professors, Pfeffer and Sutton, coined the "knowing/doing gap": the gap between ignorance and knowing is shorter than the gap between knowing and doing.[2] This theory applies to most organizations, where the gap between knowing and doing is often a chasm. OV speed bumps can be jarring enough to cause leaders to ask themselves, "Am I willing to stand up for what I believe, what I know will improve the value and long-term potential of the organization, but may decrease my status or income in the short-term?"

 Truth Bomb: The gap between ignorance and knowing is shorter than the gap between knowing and doing.

If ever you've been in the corporate board room, you know the moment when the momentum shifts back to the status quo, and the Alpha dog leader reasserts their position. The internal dialogue begins, "Should I speak up? If everyone is going left, why am I going right? What am I missing? I know the CEO said we should challenge him, but does he really want me to do that?" The prefrontal cortex formulates conflicting thoughts in nanoseconds, and just as quickly, the moment's gone, as is the opportunity to say something. The conversation has moved on. This is when you have to come fortified and ready to express your deepest convictions, regardless of the response. This takes guts, grit, and a sense of purpose that runs deeper than your desire for the next promotion or even keeping your job.

---

[2] J. Pfeffer and R.I. Sutton. 2000. *The Knowing-Doing Gap: How Smart Companies Turn Knowledge into Action.* Harvard Business Press.

When I was a teenager, I hiked up Mount McLoughlin, a volcanic mountain rising almost 9,500 feet above sea level in the Cascade Range of southern Oregon. The hike was challenging but not impossible—until the final 300 feet. The air was thin, and I was exhausted. I could see the summit, but the terrain was rocky, and my legs were shaky. I would take three steps and slide back two. It took every last bit of energy and will to persevere to the top. Creating a new path at any organization is three steps forward, two steps back. It's nights and weekends that pull you away from family and friends, not knowing if you will succeed. Many initiatives will fail. And failure can fuel the internal fortitude to press on. Failure, rejection, people thinking you're crazy—none of it will stop you when you are motivated by a deep sense of purpose. The essence of the life of an OV leader is one of continual resistance. Entrenched forces will work against you within the context of the uncertainty. People don't like uncertainty. They want assurances the new idea will be a success.

 Truth Bomb: Creating a new path at any organization is three steps forward, two steps back.

There is the "known known"—otherwise known as "sustaining innovation," where the outcome can most likely be predicted. For example, implementing a new technology requires investment, but the return is likely.

The unknown, on the other hand, can only become known through discovery. A leader simply doesn't know what they will find out, what the outcome will be. A person must be in a position to make discoveries, move forward in the darkness. This is the period known as the trough: you're putting in more effort with few or no results, probably over a long time. You resolve to be a long hauler, to see it through. Vision is not something you see; it's something you imagine until it's a reality.

What I've described as the iterative process of "observing, accepting, and acting" will be influenced by the information you don't know when you begin. That's the whole of discovery; you don't see what you're going to discover when you set out. But you do know that you're going to learn things that you don't know, and it might not be the eureka moment you want. It might be a tiny realization that causes you to move forward or change your heading. You don't really know where it's going to take you and in what timeframe. That takes a different sort of person.

Change What You Can

There is no OV without OV leaders. The first sentence of the Serenity Prayer acutely applies to leaders in the trenches doing the often thankless job of creating the next disruption: "God, grant me the serenity to accept the things I cannot change, the courage to change the things I can, and wisdom to know the difference." Every OV leader must assess the ecosystem. Some things can be impacted, and others cannot.

Satya Nadella worked at Microsoft during its trough years when it lived off its hegemonic position. Nadella was an executive vice president over its cloud and enterprise group. He had an impact on the company, but not enough to arrest Microsoft's slide. It wasn't until he was CEO that Nadella could distribute power to make the changes Microsoft needed.

Whether or not you're in an "OV company," *you* can be an OV leader. A middle manager will not be able to move the corporate needle toward OV on their own. However, a middle manager can be an example of what an OV mindset and approach looks like within their area of responsibility. Nadella was able to do that in the positions that he held before becoming Microsoft's CEO.

In the late 1990s, Nadella headed up a Microsoft program called the Value Chain Initiative to explore opportunities in end-to-end supply chains. I was a middle manager at UPS at the time, and I met Nadella at the Microsoft headquarters, pitching the concept to those of us in logistics. After hearing him tell the story of the initiative—and its promise—I got a sense for the kind of leader he would become. He had made that small Microsoft initiative his own. The Value Chain Initiative eventually was scrapped; it didn't change the company's trajectory, but Nadella used it to change his trajectory and eventually Microsoft itself.

Nadella exemplifies the OV leader who lives into the OV mindset regardless of title or position. When a middle manager does that consistently, opportunities arise. Board directors, senior managers, and top division leaders—each has a prominent role in driving OV. But there are more minor roles in a company as well: if you don't control the company or a group, control yourself. You decide how you're going to be.

Life of the Black Sheep

I loved the work at UPS. I deeply believed in its mission; I bought into its values. I was proud of what UPS did behind the scenes to prop up the communities in which it operated. I respected the people I worked with and was motivated by the number of people, both inside and outside the company, who depend on the success of UPS for their livelihood.

But I was a black sheep. I gained that reputation when I pushed against the status quo. My aspiration to bring about change at UPS sounds noble; it was gut-wrenching. And exhausting. I worked two jobs, and I got paid for one. The other required work behind the scenes—the late nights and weekends at the office.

I have always tried to drive change in every position I held. While I enjoyed some gratifying success, I failed more than I succeeded. The jobs were different, but the story unfolded in the same way. A lot of support and affirmation at the beginning, followed by resistance when I tried to apply the OV mindset to my work. The typical path was: (1) heads nodding with lots of pats on the back at the beginning, and then, (2) bitter resistance when investment without a certain outcome was needed, or existing power structures would suddenly change, or the new solution leveraged capabilities the senior leader had not yet acquired. What was gut-wrenching was not the failure. I enjoyed the learning, the discovery, and the challenge of changing hearts and minds. The OV path is not comfortable and your wins will be hard fought, but nobody changes the world managing the status quo.

I've referenced John Boyd, the OODA Loop creator, Air Force fighter pilot, and Pentagon consultant throughout this book. When he was at the Pentagon, he would always talk to new hires about a fork in the road. He would point his hand and say, "If you go that way, you can be somebody. You will have to make compromises, and you will have to turn your back on your friends. But you will be a member of the club, and you will get promoted, and you will get good assignments."

Then Boyd would point his other hand in the opposite direction: "Or you can go that way, and you can do something. Something for your country and your Air Force and yourself. If you decide you want to do something, you may not get promoted, and you may not get good assignments, and you certainly will not be a favorite of your superiors. But you won't have to compromise yourself. You will be true to your friends and to yourself. And your work might make a difference. To be somebody or to do something. In life, there is often a roll call. That's when you will have to make a decision. To be or to do? Which way will you go?"[3]

Boyd's advice was colored by the bureaucratic environment he was in. If you aspire to "do" in a status quo organization, you may be painted as a black sheep. However, in an OV organization, you can "do" something and "be" something. Doers, disruptors, and change-makers are required for OV to flourish. Find your match.

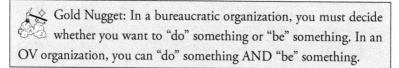

Gold Nugget: In a bureaucratic organization, you must decide whether you want to "do" something or "be" something. In an OV organization, you can "do" something AND "be" something.

Moving Past the Roadblocks

Moving up and over and around roadblocks is in large part the work of becoming an OV leader. If you are the kind to turn back at the slightest bit of resistance, you should take the fork in the road to "be" somebody. And if you want to do something, make sure you have the resolve. To create change is to embrace the life of a roadblock remover.

And yet, there is a time to move on. Every person has a limited timeline. Life is short. Your timeline is unique to you, and you can make the most of your time. Seize the moment. My moment came during my "head in hand" episode described in the Introduction. Your timeline could be based on various things, including your age, health, career goals, or opportunities with other companies. There is no "right time" other than when you decide to make a move … or not.

There are many reasons to stay: you may feel a bond with the company and people despite the frustrations. You may not want to put your family members at risk if you leave your job. It may simply be the devil you know versus the devil you don't.

I stayed at UPS well beyond the point that my Black Sheep status was certified and my career progression stalled. My wife gave me the clarity

---

[3] R. Coram. 2002. *Boyd: The Fighter Pilot Who Changed the Art of War*. Little, Brown.

I needed: "Either leave or find a way to make yourself happy where you are." I stopped thinking about where I'd been and began to focus on what I wanted to do. I applied to be a TED speaker as well as to PhD programs. I did both. I retired early from UPS in 2019 and finished my PhD. Today I am living the Act II that I dreamed of on that day of clarity.

A friend who worked in corporate strategy with me took a different path.

After enduring endless cycles of circular decision making (not saying "no" but repeatedly asking us to go back to gather more information), she reached her moment of clarity while on maternity leave. She went to a progressive online retailer, for her a match made in heaven. Today, when I speak to her, she exudes enthusiasm. She hasn't changed. The way she thinks and attacks her work is the same. She changed her environment, working for an OV company that embraces her brand of pragmatic dreaming.

If you are a CEO, you have no excuse for not being an OV company. Suppose you're an aspiring leader in an organization, perhaps a middle manager or an executive like Nadella. In that case, you may grapple with a decision to either change your organization or to change organizations. Howie Marotto, a colonel in the United States Marine Corp., told me that the Gatling gun was invented in 1862, but it took three years before it was used in combat. The technology was ready, but the military leadership was slow to change. Too often, leadership won't change until it is forced to. Suppose the leaders in your company do not have a Forever Company mindset. In that case, if they're built around quarterly advantage and not persistent advantage, you may have run up against an unmovable roadblock.

I heard Warren Buffet address a group of ambitious MBA students about 15 years ago. One young man asked, "What's the best industry for me to pursue after graduation?" Buffet replied, "Do what you love. If your heart is engaged, you will perform better and advance regardless of industry. However, all things being equal, jump on a fast-moving train, a company that is growing. An average performer on a fast-moving train will typically do better than a top performer on a slow-moving train."

There is a lesson here for CEOs and up-and-comers. If you're a CEO, make sure your organization is a fast-moving train. Eliminate the friction points and operate with OV. For the up-and-comer, you now know what to look for: a company that's accelerating. Act accordingly.

Venture into the Unknown

How Shall You Then Live?

That is the nagging, persistent question. I, personally, wrestled with it for years before my wife enlightened me. You may say, "Alan, you had a successful career at UPS." But I failed—a lot. Even in my forties, I didn't envision retiring early, completing a PhD, and writing a book on OV. What I didn't appreciate at the time was the blessing each of those experiences, both successes and failures, were. When I stopped lamenting "what could have been" and focused on "what can be," the learnings for all those experiences coalesced into new opportunities. I took stock of what I had learned and began to build snowmobiles.

There are no eight easy steps to OV. But if you analyze the characteristics of companies excelling at OV, you'll discover a competency in learning and adapting quickly. Companies go through cycles. IBM stands out as an example of continual innovation while staying committed to its core. They didn't play innovation theater. Nor did they play the safe game of sustaining innovation. Instead, they embraced disruptive innovation through an OV mindset. When IBM's mainframe business was booming, its leadership recognized that its integrated business model was fragile, so they created a services business. In 10 years, the services business was generating more than half of IBM's profits. In the mid-2000s, IBM leadership realized that the growth was in software. They acquired smaller software companies and deployed the IBM sales force to grow this segment while IBM divested its portfolio. Its market value soared. IBM's willingness to create and embrace new business models which were separate from the resource allocation and incentives of the core business is nearly impossible for most companies. When you have an 80 percent margin business, the temptation always focuses on improving what you have. But then the company misses out on the next wave.

You have the fortitude to be an OV leader. You control your own domain, whatever its size. Jump on the next wave. Choose to live. Think of all the significant decisions you've made in your life—the forks in the road. Where you would go to college, who you would marry, whether to have kids—they are all ventures into the unknown. When you jumped off the high dive, asked your secret crush to dance, or spoke up at a meeting, you crossed the chasm between knowing and doing. The key is to focus on what you can control, remain open to new learnings that challenge your understanding of the world, and then act. Live by doing.

The decision to stay and fight or leave and flourish is a profoundly personal one. At day's beginning, you wake up with yourself. Wake up *to* yourself. You cannot escape the person in the mirror. Be true to your values, your ideas, and your passion. Do something. Be something.

So how shall you then live?

What?

Operating with OV, pushing the organization continually forward, is not for the timid. This is true whether you are the CEO or a mid-level manager. Do you want to be something or do something?

So What?

The path to OV is difficult and uncertain. Making Forever Company investments may impact short-term success. The CEO will have to absorb the pressure today for a result not realized until long after their tenure. The mid-level manager will be doing two jobs, sowing existing fields while plowing new ones. That status quo is easy; change is hard. In the end, it's not about you; it's about the lives you enrich from what you do. Either at the company you are in, the company you move to, or the company you create.

Now What?

Your first step is internal, "Do you want to live?" Do you have the mindset and motivation to take the more difficult path, the path to OV, to becoming a Forever Company? If the answer is "yes," begin socializing the insights from this book on OV culture, management, structure, operations, and governance with your teams. Need help? Contact me at www.alanamling.com.

APPENDIX I

Summary of Gold Nuggets

		Page
1	Organizational Velocity is the capability to observe and accept (or not) changes in the external environment, so the firm is prepared to act best at the most appropriate time.	xxi
2	An OV company is a shark moving through the water, continually adapting to its environment.	xxiii
3	Rapid change must be met with rapid reinvention.	xxvii
4	Creating optionality is crucial for companies to thrive in a disruptive world.	7
5	You can actually be too smart and therefore sleepwalk yourself into becoming irrelevant over time.	11
6	It's not about sharpening the knife; it's about creating a new knife.	12
7	A Forever Company is in a constant state of cultural and business process reinvention.	14
8	Technology is largely a fixable problem solved with attention, creativity, and capital.	20
9	Disruption is inevitable, but the effects of disruption are not.	23
10	The digital economy requires a different kind of thinking, more like MMA fighters than Chess Masters.	25
11	Changing actions without first changing the leaders' mindset is futile because the end of the quarter is always three months away.	27

12	Companies make the mistake of thinking that there will be more casualties going on the attack than trying to defend.	35
13	You don't plan the future; you discover growth in the future.	37
14	Offense is the best defense.	38
15	It's not failing fast but learning fast—and then adapting.	39
16	Organizational Velocity is the *modus vivendi*, a way of living, for persistent advantage. Today, the only competitive advantage is to learn and react faster than your competitor—constantly. At all times.	43
17	Persistent advantage is built on optionality.	44
18	Innovation is not an idea problem, per se; it is a recognition problem.	49
19	Don't remove a fence until you know why it was put up in the first place.	52
20	OV leaders must be singularly capable of permitting the big chaos required while not being overrun by internal obstacles.	59
21	Conviction is a corporate asset.	62
22	The only failure is not learning from actions taken.	70
23	Disruption is the difference between what should happen and what does happen.	71
24	Effective leaders demonstrate all three characteristics of the Disruptor Trifecta—good judgment, know their industry, and tech-savvy.	74
25	Like any material, ideas that are too polished cannot be grasped and simply slip through one's fingers.	82
26	It's the act of verbalizing from intuition and experience that board members create new angles of thinking.	83
27	Board members must speak up; they have to challenge. Not because they don't trust the CEO, but because they do.	85
28	Ensure the board is facing disruption risk head-on by devoting one board member to focus on this area.	86
29	It's the board's job to hire the four-star general.	89

30	The board empowers management to move fast on priority actions by giving the freedom to ignore certain things.	91
31	Board members show their worth when they reach back into their intuition to frame issues facing the firm.	94
32	Board members must be in the battle, not just observers of the battle.	96
33	The new paradigm is "Trust is Given." There is no velocity without it.	100
34	Trust is like the wind, casting invisible seeds into every field of an organization.	100
35	Organizations built on trust see crazy ideas become crazy successful.	102
36	Employees looking over their shoulders are not looking ahead.	104
37	The CEO must provide conviction around the "what" and the "why" but there must be vigorous debate around the "how."	107
38	Create a virtuous circle in your organization by being transparent about the what, why, and how.	108
39	You want missionaries in your business who eat, breathe, and sleep the type of business we're in.	108
40	(What + Why) × How = Culture	109
41	The unwillingness to unwind past choices in the face of environmental change is a significant cause of friction in organizations.	111
42	Organizations without a commitment to act on outcomes will find themselves in pilot purgatory.	120
43	The genius of OV companies is that they are not trying to beat anyone at their game. Instead, they are rethinking the game entirely.	122
44	An OV leader responds to a failure by saying, "Okay, we paid the tuition, now what did we learn?"	123
45	Keep a wall around innovation, so the Mothership doesn't hug it to death.	125
46	Everyone should be a Chief Innovation Officer.	127

47	"Build snowmobiles;" take stock of your existing assets and capabilities to create new value for your customers.	136
48	As Veruca Salt drives on-demand production, the historically separate elements of manufacturing and supply chain necessarily merge.	143
49	In a bureaucratic organization, you must decide if you want to "do" something or "be" something. In an OV organization, you can "do" something AND "be" something.	158

APPENDIX II

Summary of Truth Bombs

		Page
1	The greatest source of your future success is the data that has not been created yet.	xx
2	The Internet unleashed the greatest source of power since the dawn of time, information.	xxiii
3	Success is a process, not a destination.	xxv
4	Companies get disrupted because their management is smart, not because they aren't.	2
5	Successful organizations lose to win.	5
6	Companies are never victims of disruption; they are enablers of disruption.	10
7	Business is highly personal.	13
8	Humans tend to overestimate the short-term and underestimate the long-term.	22
9	It's not a technology problem; it's a thinking problem.	22
10	The role of creating growth is the opposite of operating.	26
11	Consensus is when a group talks and talks and the person with the most power in the room says, "I think we have a consensus, and it is x."	30
12	In the absence of data, bullies and bullshitters always win.	31
13	Action must be taken before outcomes are known.	32
14	Executives need to be comfortable being uncomfortable.	34
15	Playing not to lose is the surest way to lose.	36
16	If you don't know, you know.	40
17	"That's not our business" could be the most destructive phrase in the corporate world.	42

18	You can't plan what you don't know.	47
19	All algorithms are biased.	50
20	Higher-quality inputs create higher-quality outputs.	53
21	All of us are better than any of us.	67
22	You can't give away credit, support, love—if it's done sincerely, it will come back to you.	68
23	If you're unwilling to take personal risks, you won't take corporate risks.	72
24	There are good boards, and there are bad boards.	79
25	If you're not in the boardroom, you can't conduct a proper evaluation of a board member.	92
26	A problem revealed invites solutions.	101
27	Ideas unexpressed become corporate cancer, eating away at the individual and depriving the firm of the very thing that can allow it to thrive in disruption.	101
28	Bureaucracy fights back.	113
29	Reality is already unforgivingly complex, to which disruption adds truths not yet discovered that are equally if not more complex.	117
30	Access to technology is table stakes; how firms use the technology separates the good from the great.	129
31	Industriousness and enthusiasm are the cornerstones of success.	130
32	It's lived experience that brings true diversity of thought.	132
33	We all are Veruca Salt. We want exactly what we want, when and where we want it—and at the lowest possible cost.	140
34	The time to double-down on investment is before success is obvious.	147
35	Wherever you find friction in an organization, you find a 'B' player.	148
36	You cannot affect anything or influence anyone until you first change yourself.	153
37	The gap between ignorance and knowing is shorter than the gap between knowing and doing.	154
38	Creating a new path at any organization is three steps forward, two steps back.	155

About the Author

Alan Amling, PhD, is a TED speaker and thought leader on harnessing digital disruption. Alan helped drive innovation over a 27-year career with UPS and is currently a Distinguished Fellow at The University of Tennessee and CEO of advisory firm Thrive and Advance LLC.

Index

OTHER TITLES IN THE SUPPLY AND OPERATIONS MANAGEMENT COLLECTION

Joy M. Field, Boston College, Editor

- *RFID for the Supply Chain and Operations Professional, Third Edition* by Zelbst Pamela and Sower Victor
- *Operations Management in China, Second Edition* by Craig Seidelson
- *Futureproofing Procurement* by Katie Jarvis-Grove
- *How Efficiency Changes the Game* by Ray Hodge
- *Supply Chain Planning, Second Edition* by Matthew J. Liberatore and Tan Miller
- *Sustainable Quality* by Joseph Diele
- *Why Quality is Important and How It Applies in Diverse Business and Social Environments, Volume II* by Paul Hayes
- *Why Quality is Important and How It Applies in Diverse Business and Social Environments, Volume I* by Paul Hayes
- *The Cost* by Chris Domanski
- *The Barn Door is Open* by Serge Alfonse
- *Logistics Management* by Tan Miller and Matthew J. Liberatore
- *The Practical Guide to Transforming Your Company* by Daniel Plung and Connie Krull

Concise and Applied Business Books

The Collection listed above is one of 30 business subject collections that Business Expert Press has grown to make BEP a premiere publisher of print and digital books. Our concise and applied books are for...

- Professionals and Practitioners
- Faculty who adopt our books for courses
- Librarians who know that BEP's Digital Libraries are a unique way to offer students ebooks to download, not restricted with any digital rights management
- Executive Training Course Leaders
- Business Seminar Organizers

Business Expert Press books are for anyone who needs to dig deeper on business ideas, goals, and solutions to everyday problems. Whether one print book, one ebook, or buying a digital library of 110 ebooks, we remain the affordable and smart way to be business smart. For more information, please visit www.businessexpertpress.com, or contact sales@businessexpertpress.com.